TESTIMONIES

TESTIMONIES:
a collection of lesbian
coming out stories

edited by
Sarah Holmes

Boston • Alyson Publications, Inc.

Published as a trade paperback original
by Alyson Publications
40 Plympton Street
Boston, Mass. 02118.

Distributed in the U.K. by GMP Publishers,
PO Box 247, London, N15 6RW, England.

An earlier version of Nancy Wechsler's essay, "Front Page News,"
was published in *Gay Community News* (vol. 11, no. 49).

First U.S. edition: October, 1988

ISBN 1-55583-142-7

Testimonies
editor: Tina Portillo
production and design: Wayne Curtis
proofreading: Tina Portillo
printing: McNaughton & Gunn Lithographers

Contents

Introduction

When I think about coming out as a lesbian, two major issues come to mind: the question of definition and that of visibility. Unlike our foremothers in past centuries — many of whom passed as men in order to lead the fullest lives possible, both romantically *and* sexually — we have a much wider selection of alternatives today. We are freer to define ourselves in our own terms, and then to live out our identity in an open and visible way.

Thanks to the Women's Liberation Movement, with its far-reaching impact on our consciousness, many women began to think of themselves as woman-identified, or, more to the point, as *self*-identified. Together, we could begin identifying ourselves, and while we were at it, we could finally mention the fact that we were gay women. Following and stepping on the heels of the Women's Movement was the Gay Liberation Movement, which played a major role in the coming out of many lesbians. These women chose to make themselves every bit as visible as their gay brothers as they marched and rallied beside them. And women who saw lesbians who were already "out" found the courage to step out themselves, for they suddenly had role models, a support that had previously been denied them. With the appearance of women leading openly lesbian lives, we were drawn out of our isolation and freed from the belief that we were alone.

Historically, we have been fed the lie that we as women do not have a sexuality of our own, much less a *homo*sexuality. We've been considered so irrelevant that, as far as society at large is concerned, it is unthinkable that lesbians can really exist — which shows just how heterosexualized our world really is. From our perspective, however, this is not a purely negative phenomenon, for, thanks to our invisibility, our legacy is a nice, blank page of history upon which we can now record who we are, and in great numbers.

This volume contains a cross section of lesbian coming-out experiences. Although diverse, the examples presented herein are by no means the only ways to come out. Each lesbian coming-out experience is unique, and, though many patterns seem to recur, the only truly representative anthology of this kind would have to include the story of each and every lesbian.

There are the now-common political catalysts such as those described by Angelus Bowen, who tells of her cultural identification with Audre Lorde, a black lesbian who was out of her closet and therefore a powerful role model. In was the anti-gay foster care policy of the state of Massachusetts, however, that angered Bowen into coming out publicly in 1985. She was coping with the difficulties of being a lesbian mother, and the political climate of the time gave her the impetus she needed to leave her invisibility behind.

As one who came out at a young age in the seventies, Liz O'Lexa shares some valuable insights. When she first became aware of her homosexuality at age fourteen, she was prompted to re-examine some of her attitudes regarding racism, because the object of her affection was a black girl in high school. She tells of her search for support and of feeling alienated in an established community of "mature" lesbians who didn't take her seriously and to whom she was the baby dyke underfoot. Later, she was introduced to the reality of internalized homophobia in many gay people and felt fortunate to have grown up without it.

Cookie Gant's story of growing up gay is very colorful. She describes the prostitutes who raised her and the shock she felt upon meeting her mother for the first time. Her descriptions of traumatic experiences are striking: expulsion from school for giving a present to a female schoolmate she had a crush on; being battered as a child; the racism she experienced in parochial school, along with the religious homophobic abuse she suffered as the result of being found out as a homosexual; the problem of gender identity; being committed to a mental institution at fifteen because of her homosexuality, and the initiation into gay sex she encountered there; and her attraction to prostitutes. Finally, she tells of how she met a heterosexual woman who befriended her and taught her to love and accept herself.

Several women, like Rhonda Gilliam, share with us the relief of gaining self-acceptance, no longer needing closets in which to hide from the hostility of others. Gilliam came from the Bible Belt and fell in love as a teenager with her straight best friend. After being rejected, she tried to conform to heterosexuality and was raped (Sound familiar, anyone?), after which she gave up dating. The self-hate and isolation lasted until college, when she became involved with a lesbian and they were both in a state of confusion due to religious beliefs that condemned their sexuality. Later, as a teacher, Gilliam led a double life until she was discovered in a gay bar and lost her job. She eventually found solace at the Metropolitan Community Church and support with a local gay community group.

I felt that Emma Joy Crone's story deserved inclusion in this collection because she is coming from unique places, both geographically and existentially. Having grown up and married unsuccessfully in England, she immigrated to the United States at age forty. With a background devoid of any sexual awareness and possessing no knowledge of lesbianism, she was unprepared for America's homophobic attitudes when she came out. Discovering her own feminism while in the Women's Movement, she realized that she had always had it and that all of the important relationships in her life had been with women. Today, she writes a newsletter and reaches out to other older lesbians, sharing with them the special kind of strength that it takes to come out after so many years of living in fear.

Certainly, the process of coming out has its stages, the ultimate one being that of telling loved ones, who are often the last to know. Coming out to one's parents is typically the most traumatic step in the process, which is why it is still, in many cases, avoided altogether. The responses to such disclosure cover a spectrum from the simple and easy support depicted in Jewelle Gomez's story to the extreme emotional violence of Sandra Luders being disowned, making self-acceptance an even greater struggle. Somewhere in between, we have the story Liz O'Lexa tells of her gay male friend's encouragement and support on the day she came out to her parents; after talking and crying, years later they were able to join her as she marched in her first Gay Pride Parade.

It is no small wonder that a lot of women, such as Nona Caspers, were fully practicing lesbians and *still* unaware of their gay identities. Growing up in a rural area in the sixties, Caspers enjoyed a natural intimacy with other girls, emotionally and physically, even sexually. Although she knew of no alternative to heterosexuality, she was aware that she could not have this kind of intimacy with men. So she pretended to "play" with girls, and called these sexual activities boy-girl games. When at age twenty-one she lost her virginity to a man, she believed she was heterosexual. Even though she admired lesbians, she did not identify with them. After suffering for many years with an eating disorder, she sought help in a group of women who shared her illness; there she met many other lesbians and was finally able to accept herself as one of them.

Confusion is perpetuated by society's vision of lesbianism as something merely pornographic, mainly for the pleasure of its males, rather than something that has anything to do with anybody's life. This tendency to think of lesbianism in purely sexual and male-centered terms led many lesbians to downgrade their sexuality. This is no longer the seventies, however, with coming out being so much about political movements and with the image of a true lesbian being sexless. Today there is much more room to talk about the joy of our *sexuality*, and women in this book are giving the rest of us the green light to do just that.

It is for this reason that I personally am especially grateful to Liz O'Lexa, Lisa Gravesen, Marcie Just, Gillian Hanscombe, and especially Candyce Rusk, who in their stories were not afraid to come out and claim their sexuality as fully functioning sexual beings, and even admit that it was the gay sex experience that spoke to them, saying, "This is who you are." Andrea Freud Loewenstein tells a moving tale of a week spent in the Berkshires with a woman. In her story, she relates how overwhelming the combining of sex and emotions can be.

Every one of these stories, whether of political coming-outs or those of an emotional, social, or sexual motivation, will provide more of the kind of history-book-making testimonials that we all need. They present us with reference points, different ones for each of us, to know who we are, to know that we exist in large numbers, and, above all, to know that we can be validated as very natural human beings who have historical roots of our own. And it is my hope that a reader not yet out can find the necessary strength offered by the women in these pages to take that self-affirming step.

What of other, non-lesbian readers of this volume? Welcome. Meet some of us as we are: lesbians coming out to you, bravely challenging you to see us — for we *are* your grandmothers, your mothers, your sisters, your daughters, your friends, and yes, your role models, too.

Tina Portillo
Boston, Mass.

TESTIMONIES

▼

Angelus
Cambridge, Massachusetts

Testimony

I was forty when I came out to myself. At forty-nine, I came out publicly. It sounds so simple to say "I came out." But the incremental steps along the way, the feelings and thoughts that allowed me to do that, are very clear and dear to me. The process of coming out can occur by means of little baby steps, long strides, big giant steps, and by great leaps and bounds. I've had experience with all of these.

When I fell deeply in love with a woman at the age of forty during the mid-70s, I didn't question for even a second that I was a lesbian. My emotional connections had always been with women, and two light affairs spread over the previous twenty years had let me know that sexual relationships with women were exciting. Neither time had I suffered angst over it — I just accepted it as one part of my nature. But suddenly at forty, I knew what all the songs and poetry were about. I was delighted to finally have myself figured out.

It was important for me to discover out lesbians, but even more so to discover black lesbians willing to be out. I wanted more than anything to be able to be completely out in the Connecticut city where I was living then. However, it wasn't safe for me, my business, or my family. During that period, I saw Audre Lorde speak, and heard her siren call: "What are the silences that you swallow day by day?" she asked. "If we wait to speak until we are not afraid, we will be sending messages back from the grave," she said. I knew then that I would live my life as an open lesbian as soon as I was able. I began working to extricate myself from my complicated heterosexual family life so that I could write and speak exactly as I wanted to.

Six years after hearing Lorde's fateful exhortation, I moved to Cambridge to join my lover (not the one I fell in love with at forty). Aside from the desire to live in a politically active community, I was also drawn by the blood family on both sides that my two children could experience. My ex-husband and I were born and raised in Boston, where some of our siblings still lived, which gave my children instant access to relatives, including an eighty-year-old paternal grandmother. Since I never had grandparents, I wanted them to experience her as much as possible while they had the chance. It was a wise decision; she died three years later. That period of time spent nurturing the bond between my children and their grandmother (especially my daughter, who was ten when we moved) was also spent learning to do several things: work for another agency besides my own for the first time in more than twenty years; live as a fairly anonymous member of a community; discover whether writing skills used sparingly for more than a quarter of a century could still work for me.

When I first began writing for the Boston women's newspaper *Equal Times*, anyone reading my first article carefully might have made the assumption that I was a lesbian. It was about "Les Ballets Trockadero," a group of male ballet dancers who dressed in tutus and toe shoes and acted female as well as male parts. My ardent plea for eliminating sex roles in ballet might have been a tip-off, if not an outright giveaway. Some of my later pieces for *Bay Windows* and *Sojourner* might also have led one to believe that I was a lesbian. For instance, in one particular *Bay Windows* piece on presidential candidates addressing women's issues, my closing comment was a lament that in listing the various constituencies of women these candidates had to be concerned with, no one had the temerity to bring up lesbians. Of course, all my women's community friends "knew for sure" about me. But I'd never said it publicly or in print. Then in May 1985 the foster care issue hit the gay community.

(In May 1985 Massachusetts Governor Michael Dukakis instituted a policy in the Department of Social Services effectively banning lesbians and gay men from being foster parents.)

The Gay and Lesbian Defense Committee held several meetings which I attended, relating my experience as a lesbian foster mother. As Gay Pride Day approached in June, I was called and asked to speak at the rally on the Boston Common about this experience.

That's when I first realized that I had not been as out as I'd thought, because when I told my life partner that I'd been asked to speak, she expressed fear for me. Somewhat puzzled, I stated that since everybody knew anyway, I didn't know what the problem was. She made me realize that nowhere had I actually stated publicly that I was a lesbian. I was astonished, but it was true. My first flip response was, "Well, then, what better place to do it? Fifteen thousand people can hear it at once, then there certainly can't be any doubt." We discussed for a couple of days the dangers of being out in the larger community versus the relative safety of being a lesbian in the women's community. She expressed her fears for me, herself, and the children (a boy who was seventeen at that time, and a girl of eleven). I also took that time to let my children know that this speech was going to happen. It did and it was a tremendous experience.

The decision to speak to that many people on Boston Common was very scary. But, like Audre Lorde, like Barbara Smith, like Beverly Smith . . . women I had read and admired during my closet days . . . I wanted to be out there for that lone black woman who might need to see me at a significant time in her life.

Sometimes we throw ourselves out there and we're never really sure whom we're affecting. But I've had good feedback. One closeted black woman who didn't feel safe enough to come to the rally saw a tape of my Gay Pride speech on cable. She taped it herself, and then managed to meet up with me later. She said she was so surprised and glad to see my black face that she almost kissed the TV screen. Another closeted woman came to a lesbian workshop I did on Cape Cod as part of a conference by women who had been to the women's conference in Nairobi and she said she never even imagined that the woman leading the workshop was going to be black. Both these women were as relieved to discover me as I was to discover them, and we have formed ongoing friendships. A relative of mine recently called to say she had just discovered her son is gay and she needed to discuss her feelings and talk about how to handle it. Everything is fine with them now, and I'm delighted I was out there so that she could have someone to turn to.

These are only some of the positive reactions to my being such an out black lesbian. However, lest you think this is an entirely altruistic undertaking, I must say unequivocally that I'm having absolutely the grandest, most affirming and uplifting time I've ever had. Finally, I feel all together — whole and happy.

My dreams at age forty didn't even begin to prepare me for the freedom I feel at age fifty. So, for anyone shackled in some closet with the door locked, I say, "Keep picking at the lock." No matter how long it may take, you deserve to know this feeling, even if it's for only one day before you die.

This piece and the speech that follows are connected not only in theme but also in feeling, in the manner of "testifying." Taken together, I call them "Testimony."

Gay Pride Speech
June 15, 1985 on Boston Common

Hello. I'm Angela Bowen, a mother and writer, and I'm very happy to be here today. I'd like to tell you a story.

When I was a young married woman with a year-old baby, I moved with my husband to Connecticut to open a dancing school. One day a social worker called to ask if I could find something for a fourteen-year-old girl to do in exchange for dancing lessons. We met, she started baby-sitting for our son, and eventually began staying late for dinner, and on into the evening, obviously hating to return to her foster home at night. When I finally won her confidence, I found out she was being physically abused by the woman, who used to beat her with a broom handle, and sexually abused at night by the fifty-five-year-old man of the house, an elder in his church, by the way. I told the social worker, who asked us to take her into our home. After weeks of persuading a very reluctant husband, and months of looking for a larger apartment so she could have her own room, I succeeded in gaining a new foster daughter. She lived with us until she was grown, and is now a thirty-five-year-old mother of two. She says I gave her the first respect and sense of family she'd had in years. We're still good friends.

Two years after she came to live with us, my husband's first wife died and his eleven-year-old daughter came to live with us. I legally adopted her, and we raised her until she was grown. She's thirty now, and the mother of a ten-year-old daughter.

I was always the main parent of all the children in our house — but when I took in that foster daughter, I was a new mother with an infant, and I was only twelve and a half years older than the teenager I was raising. But that was okay with the state of Connecticut; they pestered, they called and kept on pressing for the placement while I was trying to convince my husband, and looking for a new apartment so the child could have a room of her own. I don't recall any examination, but the social worker was extremely impressed with us: the ideal heterosexual couple with a little baby, and just beginning a business. We'd had no experience with raising children, but — no problem — we'd learn.

The judge who awarded the adoption decree for my stepdaughter also thought we were pretty ideal. He especially commented on my strong character. No problem. You see, I was straight, so I had to be okay.

But now, five children later (and after having taught a few thousand as well), if I applied to the Department of Social Services in Massachusetts, I couldn't get a foster child. I'm unfit, says the state. Everything's changed because now I'm aware that I love women. So, all the experience I've gained would mean nothing next to that of a young woman just starting out, as long as she had the shadow of a man beside her, whatever his character, willing or unwilling to open his heart to a child, or lying in wait to assault that child, with his cover of heterosexual respectability saving him from the slightest scrutiny. That's how this homophobic society wastes its resources by throwing us away and wiping out our lives.

What I want to talk about is the potential solidarity this awful incident offers to us all. If some of us have felt alienated from one another, for whatever reasons, all the various factions of the gay and lesbian community can feel solidarity on this one issue, at least; as can all our principled straight friends, families and political allies.

I can stand up here saying these things because my children are biologically and legally mine, so I'm not in danger of losing them. I also know that whenever sick-minded political opportunists decide to, they can legislate that biological children are endangered by their parents' homosexuality or lesbianism. They won't even need a complainant — just the law. If they come for you tonight and I don't stand with you, they'll be back for me tomorrow. Not one of us is safe, in or out of our closets, until each one of us is legally protected.

We were proud enough to come out today to honor ourselves and our own choices. Some of us barely out, scared, but here. Some stepping a bit more firmly each year, and some of us *waaay* out there. For myself, I've been sticking my head further out each year, but I feel daring and proud today because I'm speaking for the first time as an openly lesbian woman. Yes, we're gay and we're proud and I'm so happy for all of us smart enough to have figured out our way past all the obstacles thrown up to prevent us from finding our natural partners in our own particular order of the universe. But let's also be smart enough to get together and *fight* — not only for ourselves, but for all those children waiting hopefully for loving homes that we've already proved we can provide.

Whatever comes, let's get ready and stay ready. They don't know who they're messing with. Not *yet*, anyway.

▼

Nona Caspers
Minneapolis, Minnesota

Home

For me there was no one clinch-
ing moment, mad love, or political leap that landed me in Lesbos.
Coming out to myself and to others was a matter of finding a way
to survive and letting myself thrive.

I was one of those wispy white-haired girls, born into rural
Minnesota, Catholicism, and the sixties. My strong legs were
wrapped in itchy pink tights and hidden under synthetic frills. I
remember twirling round and round in the driveway, with my
long hair flying, and skirts flapping like feminine flags. I was
happy. I had a neighborhood full of Catholic girlfriends. We
played S.P.U.D., Annie Annie Over, Wonder Bread Commun-
ion, Chinese Sticks, dolls, and another game we called Tickle. We
would climb four at a time, one on each pole of a swingset, mish-
mashing our vulvas against the metal until a tickle rooted between
our legs and sprouted throughout our blessed bodies. We giggled
and talked to each other the whole time. Vicky, Beth, or Lisa's
face hung across from mine. It was an intimate, soothing and
sacred girl ritual.

Then there was Romeo and Juliet — we took turns being one or the other. We held hands and kissed, passionately twisting our lips together like Steve and Rachel on *Another World*. I remember the times we slept at each other's houses, and cuddled up close like two chips melting together. And we'd talk; intense, excited talk that mixed our thoughts and feelings together like dough.

I felt safe and warm during those years. The closeness, these friendships, were what life was all about. Nobody said anything to me about the touching. We were just little girls — playing.

By the seventh grade, with breasts and blood approaching, my childhood safety had disappeared. In my rural high school the "sexual revolution" meant girls felt more pressure, called freedom, to revolve around the penis. While the church encouraged my "safe" friendships with girls, the coolest, bravest deed was to touch a boy. I started to hang out with the most heterosexually active girls. We would sit nose to nose, knee to knee, whispering, with my long hair floating between our intense faces. Our words and voices mingled, rose and fell. Our closeness depended on telling every detail. I had nothing to tell. Certain boys made me nervous and I took these feelings to be crushes. But I would rather be with my girlfriends talking about it than with those boys, doing something about it — and for all their boy-crazy activity, they did too.

As the pressure increased I became extremely anxious. I began to sense that there was something wrong with me. Not the usual zit on the tip of my nose or the "tell-me-the-truth-am-I-weird" insecurities of adolescence. I felt a cold white secret, a longing, lodged beneath my rib cage. I had to guard this spot from everyone, even myself. I acted like a tough femme — seductive, confident. I entertained my girlfriends by getting into trouble; sassing at teachers, running loud, wild and bold. I remember sneaking apples from a yard we passed during our daily phys-ed run and giving them to my newest close friend Carrie. Teachers kicked me out of classes and told me to "act like a lady." Although my girlfriends admired my guts, I felt scared every minute of every day, as though at any time some filth would spill out of me, rolling and clanging on the streets for everyone to see. The only part I could name was the fear.

I became preoccupied with trying to figure out how I would ever be in a heterosexual relationship as there seemed to be no other kind. The intimacy and emotional attachments with girl-friends, and later, women friends, came so easily and felt so natural and fulfilling. Intimacy felt so impossible, so utterly out of reach and dangerous with men. Yet, in the world I grew up in, heterosexuality was inevitable. The only women I had ever known that got out of it were nuns. I did *not* want to be a nun.

I remember two isolated and very buried incidents in my teen years, when my emotional attractions became sexualized. Carrie invited me over to her house, seven miles from my hometown of Melrose, Minnesota. I remember being very excited. I dressed carefully, brushed my long blonde hair until the brush bristles sagged, and accentuated my breasts. I thought of her breasts, how they had popped out and were so fleshy and firm. A hope dug its way to the surface of my thoughts, with a vague wish that something might happen and Carrie might want to play.

We were sitting in her older sister's car, going through her purse, when we found a flat round pill box with the days of the week printed on it. Carrie asked me if I knew what they were. I did. We sat quiet a long time, and the air thickened. Then she asked me if I wanted to play a boy/girl game. I acted dumb and said, "Sure," praying to the Catholic God I'd grown up with that she meant what I thought. She did. I remember clearly how our bodies folded so comfortably together. I felt warm and safe — like home. I thought it couldn't last. It could only be practice for the real thing. We were just playing.

The next time we were sexual was two years later. As she invited me, she said that she knew two boys, Kenny and Bob, who would meet us at a café. I was anxious and felt sick, but I wanted to be with her, to talk and talk and laugh into the night. My stomach pains went away when the boys didn't show up and we returned to her house. Finally we lay in bed and I pretended to be asleep. My skin tingled as I wished that she would touch me. She did. I stayed half asleep, not daring to respond as she moved my hands over her breasts. I mumbled, "Kenny"; she whispered, "Bob." In the morning we could not look each other in the eye. We both said, "I had a dream about a boy."

Soon after this dream I made a few drugged, drunken attempts to connect with the other gender. Boys liked me, but I didn't seem to care about them. I retreated into starvation and obsessive exercise. I whittled away my female flesh, my anger, my fears, my sexuality. My goal in life was to be able to wear my twelve-year-old brother's Levis. I did. I was sixteen.

When I was twenty-one I was hiding two things — my eating patterns and my virginity. At times I lied. I had avoided contact with men as much as possible, continuing to seek out close women friends wherever I went. But enough was enough, I told myself. If I could hike alone through Guatemala, climb volcanos, live in a teepee and out of a van, put up eleven cords of wood and get A's in chemistry, then surely I could develop a "normal" emotional and sexual relationship with a nice man.

I picked Doc. We were both planting trees in the South. He turned out to be gay, or "bisexual with a heavy emotional inclination towards men." After our first bout of intercourse he asked me if I was a lesbian. I laughed and said, "No," with confidence.

Lesbians were somebody else. Lesbians were the women in the lesbian section of *Our Bodies, Ourselves* — women with short hair and caps, standing together with arms across shoulders, hands cupping each other's breasts — those were lesbians. The scenes in *Going Down with Janice*, Peggy Castenada's unscrupulous book which I read secretly in high school — that was lesbianism. Kim, a girl in high school who carved her name into her arm and gifted me with stolen incense burners before she ran off to California, and then called me up and told me she had a wife — she was a lesbian. A lesbian was a woman who had sex with women, who craved sex with women, who creamed her jeans whenever she was with women — I didn't; I wasn't. I creamed my jeans for no one.

Ironically, I held some admiration, awe and respect for lesbians. As an ex-Catholic, I held onto the feeling that somehow it was better to fool around with women than to be defiled by men. Being lesbian was close to being a nun. Lesbians were different; sometimes they looked comfortable, playful, happy, and independent. At other times I saw them as fad hoppers, immature and ill. Mostly I didn't think of them at all and neither did anyone else I knew.

I decided I had found love with Doc. I nurtured and protected my fantasy of being with him, not caring that he had "emotional homosexual tendencies." There was nothing wrong with that. But whenever I was with him I felt lonely, irritable, and needy. My eating patterns got worse. I was exhausted and cold. I thought that all I needed, for my sanity and to fulfill my heterosexual fantasy, was to get well.

I moved to Minneapolis, Minnesota and began to attend a Women's Eating Disorder Group. The women in the group were creative, independent, and also afraid. Soon after joining the group I caught on that half of them were lesbians. I had dinner at a couple's house and saw how loving and how "normal" they were. In the group we talked more and more about how our food problems related to being female in a female-hating world. We were being controlled through myths and values about weight. Our energy to create, question, and fight back was drained or diffused by our focus on food and the constant public reference to our bodies and our appearance. We talked about the cycle of starving and binging as an escape from the expectations put upon traditional femininity. Then I made a very special friend, Julie.

Julie was never my lover, but she was the first woman I thought about being lovers with. She was a real girlfriend and together we explored the idea that we could, if we wanted to, be lesbians.

Gradually, as I became familiar with more lesbians and aware that a lesbian culture did exist, I began remembering and understanding my childhood and adolescence. And I began to relax. There was a place for me. I did not have to force myself to be with men. I was lesbian. I was home.

I have identified myself as a lesbian for five years. I have been "well" for about that long. I was in a relationship for two years and am now preparing to date. The first time my ex-sweetheart and I played was like a warm, safe trip into a time when I was whole. Everyone in my ten-person German Catholic family knows. When I recently told my still-Catholic sister, with my heart pounding, she smiled and said, "I was wondering if you were ever going to tell me."

▼

Alana Corsini*
New York, New York

Loving Jenny

We met during our first year of college. There were four of us; four young women who wanted to be actresses, writers, painters, or dancers. We were at college during the Vietnam era, and while we were politically and socially involved in our times, it was our shared artistic dream that bound us together. Surprisingly, twenty years later, we have all achieved a version of our early dreams. Jenny and Tilly are actresses who work in television and film in Los Angeles, Mona is a Bay Area painter with regular shows, and I spend a lot of time at my word processor in New York spewing forth novels, poems, plays, screenplays, and articles on the arts.

No self-respecting aspiring artist or intellectual joined sororities in those days, so the four of us rented an old "railroad" apartment a mile from campus. It had three bedrooms and a glassed-in front porch, which allowed each of us to have a private room. The wallpaper in the dining room featured a grey feather motif against a bland background the color of an internal organ, and the living room couch was supported on one side with empty coffee cans filled with pebbles. It was heaven. I claimed the large bedroom which could accomodate my double bed covered with an obligatory Indian-print bedspread. I had a huge slate-top desk, a bookcase filled with poetry and esoteric, occult philosophy, and an ancient radiator spray-painted a dull gold. I thought the room struck just the right note between intellectual and erotic.

The late sixties and early seventies was touted as an era of great sexual freedom, although this freedom was bounded by the presumption of heterosexuality. Given that one provision, anything else was acceptable. Mona fell in love with the graduate student upstairs, and lived with him for years before they married. Tilly went in for serial monogamy. Sex was something she fit in between rehearsals, callbacks, and career planning.

Jenny and I, however, entered the sexual olympics with great vigor during our college years. It required the skills of an air traffic controller to orchestrate the comings and goings of our various lovers. Jenny ran the gamut from a sweet, stuttering fraternity boy to an Italian rock musician she met in Milan to a middle-aged millionaire playboy. I did my part with a bisexual actor, assorted professors (I was an intellectual groupie), a rotund hospital administrator, and an angelic theological student who was losing faith in the grip of illicit sex.

Homosexuality to me, at that time, was associated with ancient Greece, modern French literature, and one openly gay Arab actor I knew in school. As far as it pertained to women, I knew about Gertrude Stein, tough dykes in motorcycle jackets, and Collette's experiences in boarding school. And I considered myself sophisticated.

When we graduated in 1971, our core of four dissolved. Only Jenny and I got degrees — Mona was already off with Ron at another university, and Tilly had dropped out to take up a great career opportunity and got married quickly and quietly to her first husband.

I went off to New York to work for a peace/environmental agency by day and an off-Broadway producer by night. It was a lonely year. I had two or three affairs with men I didn't care about, and yearned for the closeness I had had with friends. Jenny was with an improvisational comedy troupe, and we corresponded constantly by letter and tape. Through the months our exchanges became tinged with longing, loss, and a feeling that in our new lives no one knew us as authentically as we knew each other.

After a year in New York, I impulsively decided to move to Hawaii with two male friends from college and passed through Chicago to say good-bye to my family and whatever friends were still around. I had a strong need to see Jenny and arranged to spend a week with her before leaving for my Pacific adventure.

During the seven-hour drive I found myself in a state of nervous excitement, belting out torch songs Jenny and I used to sing in college. It was to be a homecoming and an adventure all in one. Jenny. I hadn't seen her in almost a year and there was nobody I wanted to see more.

Jenny was living in an apartment in an old white frame house with a roommate named Karen, an actress and auto mechanic who carried her own set of vw tools wherever she traveled as a sort of insurance policy against the vicissitudes of theatrical life. When I arrived, Jenny was alone in the apartment, and I was happy for the rare opportunity to have her to myself. She was a Leo and a born entertainer, and tended to gather crowds around her.

At six feet, Jenny had a flair for theatrical costume. She concocted outfits from thrift shop castoffs, strings of beads, and scarfs that suggested a moving caravan. Other times she'd wear a military or pea coat and stocking cap to create an image of Verushka playing Billy Budd. This day she stood before me unadorned, wearing plain blue slacks and an Oxford cloth shirt. Her blonde hair — which had been rinsed a unique orange-pink shade during her summer modeling in Italy and only now was halfway returned to its natural color — was shorn close to her head. Mannish, I thought, and felt a lurch in my stomach as we hugged and held each other close for a long moment.

We were both physical people; huggers and embracers and touchers, but for the first time there was awkwardness between us. It must have been the long separation, I thought fleetingly. Then we plunged into our stories over countless cups of coffee, and all strangeness vanished. We knew each other. We loved each other. We had years of shared crisis and jubilation and insight and growing up in common. Everything would be fine, I thought.

But it wasn't. The strangeness returned; the strain in the air, the uncomfortable silences. For two days I followed Jenny around in her life. Was it my imagination, or did she purposely keep other people near us most of the time? I went to rehearsals with her. We ate most meals with the other actors, and Jenny had the troupe over to the apartment both nights. There was singing and good humor and rarely a private moment.

Finally, very late and long after Karen had gone to bed, Jenny and I would tumble into her bedroom and drop, exhausted, onto her waterbed and fall asleep. Although I had never seen her room before, it felt familiar. She had the wire sculpture from her college room on the wall opposite the bed, and strings of beads and baubles were looped over chairs and racks. I was conscious of keeping my body from touching Jenny as we slept, not wanting to . . . to what?

I was miserable. Jenny would start to give me a delicious massage on the undulating waterbed, then abruptly jump up to make coffee. Or she'd draw me a hot bubble bath and call me into the bathroom, only to avert her eyes and rush out of the room when I slipped into the water. Something was definitely wrong.

On the third day Jenny left at midmorning for rehearsal and asked me to meet her at the local pizza parlor for lunch. I laid around most of the morning reading poetry and writing in my journal in an effort to figure out exactly what was going on. I was off to Hawaii on a great adventure, but how come I wasn't thrilled and raring to get going? I decided that it was useless to hang around with Jenny any longer. Maybe now that we were out of college we didn't have that much in common any more. She was so involved with the theater and her actor friends, there didn't seem to be much room for me. Sharing a past doesn't guarantee a continued closeness, I reasoned. I'd just tell Jenny at lunch that I needed to get a lot of things cleared up in Chicago before I left, and that I couldn't stay the entire week as I had originally planned. She'd understand. We'd always be friends and keep in touch.

Once the decision was made my mood took a decided turn for the better. I gathered my books together and packed my bag before I started out for the restaurant. I smiled and hummed a tune as I strolled down the street. For the first time I was aware of the delicate intricacies of the tree branches above me.

When I arrived Jenny was sitting alone in the corner, resting her elbows on the edge of a table covered with a red-checked cloth. I sat down, brimming with my newly found good humor, and ordered pizza and a Coke. I felt light and at ease and chatted a good deal about nothing in particular. Jenny's face started to brighten. She commented on how I seemed like my old self once again and laughed in her easy, generous way. I was about to tell her that I was leaving that afternoon when I caught the sudden intensity of her gaze. The smile gently faded from Jenny's face. Our eyes locked on each other, and my heart turned over in my chest. I recognized the look in Jenny's luminous brown eyes and the hot feeling coursing through my body. Desire. We both felt it. And we both knew it.

To this day, I don't remember who spoke first, but I remember the simple question, "Do you want to go?" Knives and forks came to rest noiselessly on the edges of plates. Dollar bills drifted onto the table. We walked out of the restaurant back to the apartment and directly into Jenny's bedroom in a slow-motion, soft-focus daze. We started to undress singly, then turned to undress each other, shyly at first. We were both comfortable undressing our male lovers and we were both comfortable with each other. But to undress your best friend as you did a lover was very new. Didn't seduction depend at least in part on unfamiliarity?

We rolled on to the waterbed and I thrilled to the feel, the smell and touch of Jenny. Softness, tenderness, and such overwhelming passion. I was half dizzy. We rubbed, we rolled, we laughed, and finally we shared wondrous tears. Jenny claimed that now she understood why men were so hooked on women's breasts. I suddenly understood that my entire life had changed.

Jenny and I were lovers. All sorts of emotions erupted in me. I, who had been so blasé about my boyfriends, became fiercely jealous of anyone who paid attention to Jenny. When she performed and I saw a man leer appreciatively at her from the audience I had the urge to turn the table over in his lap and scream, "Back off, you creep, she's coming home with *me.*" Ah, yes. Cool, intellectual Alana transformed into Anna Magnani on a rampage. In my muddled state of wonder, I gave little thought to any future, but as the week wore on, Jenny forced me to recognize some hard realities.

Being a lesbian did not appeal to her, Jenny confessed one morning as we were sipping coffee in the kitchen. It had taken her so long to believe that she was attractive to men, and she wasn't ready to throw it all away. And she didn't think she could stand to be an outcast, either. I was stunned. The word lesbian had not been formed yet in my own mind. We could both continue to see men, I offered. We both liked men, didn't we? Except we'd have each other as well. Jenny was evasive. Wasn't I about to move to Hawaii? Yes, but that could be changed. After all, everything seemed to have been made new in the past few days. No, Jenny felt that we should each go on with our own lives. Stunned, I had nothing else to say. It was clear that whatever the future was to be, it could not contain the two of us as lovers.

And so, when the week was out, I drove back to Chicago, sold my car and flew to Hawaii to meet my friends. Slowly, I accepted the fact that while Jenny loved me, she was not a lesbian, and that her life was going to evolve separately from mine. This affair with Jenny put me in touch with my feelings for women. For years I see-sawed between men and women before realizing that while it is easy to get in and out of bed with either sex, what is deepest in me is touched only by another woman.

Sometimes I don't see Jenny for years, but every few months we exchange a long letter or half-hour phone call. She sends me photos of her husband's paintings and of their children — blond, and tall as Hitler Youth, she has commented dryly. I send her manuscripts and pictures of me with my lover and our animals. I watch her on television; she reads my work. We still care.

We never mention the week fifteen years ago when we were lovers. I don't even know if her husband knows about our affair, but I suspect that he'd think it was fine. I wonder, sometimes, if Jenny thinks about our interlude at all, and if so, how she remembers it. I know that, at that time, being a lesbian touched a place of fear in Jenny. I wonder if now that she is secure in herself she'd remember it as a time of "rounding out" her sexual education, as an expression of love for a friend, or as the satisfaction of a curiosity.

Maybe the next time Jenny and I are both on the same coast at the same time I'll ask her how she feels about it. And then again, maybe I won't. Her response could not alter in me the bright, bittersweet memory, nor the quiet joy, that continues to come from loving Jenny.

* *a penname has been used to assure the author's anonymity*

▼

Emma Joy Crone
British Columbia, Canada

Crone Story

For me, coming out has been a continuous, growing, empowering experience — not something I can intellectualize, but a political, philosophical, and emotional way of life.

1968 found me in San Francisco, long before it became the city of freedom for homosexuals that it is today. I was newly divorced after twelve years of marriage, newly immigrating, looking for a new husband, and not at all interested in the feminist movement which was in full swing around me. I was resisting the suggestions by my friend Louise that I "go to a Women's Meeting." I did not want to be one of those women wearing blue jeans; I was forty years old and thought I was pretty set in the way of life that I had known all those years. However, I had always been a political being, and the fact that the invasion of Cambodia was happening and much was developing around this issue in the U.S. at that time, prompted me to go with others from my place of work to a workshop entitled "Women and Work" in Berkeley. At this workshop, a feminist (unrecognizable as such to me because of my preconceptions) talked of what was happening on campus around women's issues. Doors flew open in my head, and on returning to my place of work I announced to my friend Louise that I was interested in going to a consciousness-raising group. One visit, and I knew that I had always been a feminist — little did I realize that this was to be my first step to coming out.

My life up to this time had been spent in an industrial city in England. I had never heard the word lesbian, but as a young woman someone pointed a pub out to me where "those women" went. When I asked what this meant, my friend said, "If you go in there and sit down, they will come and talk to you and touch you on the leg" — this was my basic introduction to lesbianism. I didn't hear the word until I became involved in women's issues. Never before had I been exposed to any of the depressing, sad, inhibitory, homophobic stories I have heard since then. Sex when I was growing up meant babies, nothing more. As with many people of my generation, the joys of sensuality or sexuality with either sex were never made known to me, let alone the fact that I could enjoy my life as a woman loving women in a way totally unimagined to me.

On looking back now, it feels to me that my immigration to the U.S. at the age of forty was the real beginning of my life. My first three months were spent in the city of New York. What an experience! My life as a heterosexual in a repressive culture of working-class attitudes towards life and marriage had left me totally unprepared for the attitudes and openness I found working in one of the largest cancer research establishments as a floating secretary. The first office I worked in was with a gay man and a woman of color who thought I was a hoot because of my English expressions, and learning the American language proved to be a constant challenge of new expressions and misuse of words, such as "rubber" for "eraser." The other difference which to me at that time was very important was the attitude towards divorce. In England, I had literally been shunned as a divorced woman in places I worked, and felt I had failed in this aspect, then important to me, of my life as a woman. However, in the U.S., the reaction was "Is it your third or your fourth divorce?" I was stunned, and while nowadays I have a very different outlook on this attitude towards marriage, at the time it was a very freeing experience. My background had been one where one kept the marriage vows and did not look at another man (let alone woman), and I can only now see that my marriage was a very dull and forbidding experience in my life.

I stayed in New York for three months; on hearing of the awful winters they experienced there, I decided to take a plane to sunny California. Incidentally, I should say at this point that during the whole of this adventure I knew no one in the United States. I had taken off from England in a very sad, depressed state, convinced my life was over, and that I would just find another husband and hey, presto, all would be well.

San Francisco at first was not too exciting: jobs were hard to find, and agencies were charging large fees to put one in touch with an employer. I lived in a Catholic hostel for women, this being the cheapest place to find that provided huge breakfasts, part of which I would take to work with me for lunch! I finally found work in a large teaching hospital, and it was there that I met Louise. We worked in the same department, had coffee breaks and lunch together, and spent many weekends at either her home or mine. Everyone was talking about us, waiting for "it" to happen.

Once I had discovered myself as a feminist I then became involved in many sharing womanly projects that were happening around me. It was a time of great excitement and opening up for me, as for many other women at this time: skills taught by women, art, meetings, self-defense classes, and my empowerment around the issue of rape. Women were opening their homes to do projects in. I met many wonderful women, but my awareness that I was mixing with lesbians did not come till much later. Louise and I used to go to gay bars, as well as hang around with lots of women. In those days there was no Amelia's or Mama Bear's or coffeehouses for women. We just sat watching at the women's dances we went to, never dancing together, until one night when we finally decided to try it out. I must mention at this time that, though feminist and involved with all these women-oriented happenings, we were still relating to, and sleeping with, men. I cannot believe nowadays that I can have been so naive as to not realize that many of the women with whom we related were lesbians. No one ever tried to initiate us into lesbianism — contrary to societal belief about homosexuality.

One day Louise and I were out driving, and right out of the blue I said to her, "Have you ever wondered what it would be like to make love with a woman?" She gripped the steering wheel hard.

"I don't know," was all she answered, with no more discussion.

She was extremely quiet for the rest of the day, and I felt I had made a *faux pas* and did not pursue the subject. I had no idea where my question was coming from. We'd neither of us during our growing up time had the freedom to express our needs, sexual or otherwise. So discussions around sexuality were still taboo, and as I've said before, relating in a sexual way to women was something neither of us had heard of. Louise, who was also forty, had been brought up Roman Catholic, and my upbringing, though not religious, had been completely devoid of any knowledge about sexuality.

One weekend when I was home in bed on a Saturday night, there was a knock on the door. Louise and our gay male friend had just been to Kelly's Bar (this was in San Francisco, forty-five miles away — I was living in Sonoma County), and had decided to drop in and see me. We talked a while (it was midnight) and then a discussion as to where to sleep ensued. The gay man decided on a piece of foam on the floor, and Louise to jump into bed with me. We were neither of us prepared for what happened, for that night I caressed a woman for the first time in my life. We didn't make love in the sense of genital sex, but we realized we were women loving each other. The next morning I was overwhelmed with delight, for not only could I be close with women as a feminist, but I could actually be lovers with women. I wanted to shout from the housetops; it was the most wonderful, amazing thing that had ever happened to me.

I was so elated with this new aspect of my life that on going to work the following Monday, I rushed into a department where I knew a young lesbian technician, and I burst out with my news. Then came my first introduction to homophobia. "Hush," she said. "You mustn't tell everyone, people don't like us." Back then I could not understand why; since then I have learned much about society's attitudes. To this day I am not ashamed. I have no sense that there is anything wrong in my being a lesbian; it feels the most natural way of life to me. If people don't like who I am, they don't have to relate to me. There are many wonderful lesbians in the world, so I don't feel the loneliness that many lesbians in the past have had the misfortune to experience.

I have met many lesbians while traveling in Europe and living on women's land in the United States, Denmark, England, and Canada, where I now live.

One of my greatest coming out experiences was in Oregon, where in 1977 I went to a Gathering of Older Women (I was forty-nine at the time) happening in Wolf Creek. I went to find my peers, and there discovered myself as a writer, a spiritual woman, and, most exciting of all, a countrywoman. I had never thought I could once again find a new lifestyle and one that was more conducive to my way of living and happiness than I had yet experienced. I learnt many new skills (once again from women); I learned that I did not have to have bulging muscles to chop wood, and that I had peer counseling skills. Other women showed me how I hid my fears, and how to be a real person in my relationships with women. I felt safe to explore myself as a human being, letting go once again of many misconceptions about myself. Many workshops and many months later, I returned to Canada filled with a sense of selfhood. In Oregon I formed non-sexual relationships with many new women who have since become my "family," but I call them my tribe. These lesbians now live in many parts of the world, and I have a tribal family with whom I keep in constant contact. It sure beats the life experience I had before the age of forty.

Country living has become for me the life I want to live for as long as I am on this planet. I see this as coming from my childhood, for when I was growing up in a smoggy, polluted city, I used to escape to the countryside, youth hosteling every weekend. The youths I was with, on looking back, were always women. I see that my life has constantly been woman-oriented, and though I never thought about it until writing this, I, like many others, went through the "crushes" on two of my schoolteachers — one the gymmistress (as they were then known) and the other my English teacher, who, I remember, had beautiful red hair and was called Miss Frost (sigh). Country life has meant that I have time to develop my skills without city distractions. I am busier than I have ever been. While always being open to challenge and learning more about myself and the world around me, I feel this is the reason that lesbianism is not hard for me. I love life, and at sixty years old, which I am now, I feel I am entering new phases, new beginnings. I recently had my first article published, I am working on watercolors, and I am taking drawing lessons. For the past four years I have been putting out a newsletter aimed at increasing the visibility of older lesbians, hoping that this would encourage others to share their life experiences, dreams, and visions of alternatives for their future as elders to those presented by current society.

I live on one of the Gulf Islands of British Columbia, and while this can be isolating, I fill my time adequately. I have now been celibate for three years, by choice. This is not because I no longer want to love and be with women, but because I am going through a healing process — for with awareness comes the understanding of what I have been doing with most of my life, some of which has of course been quite hard to cope with. In particular, I think of menopause, that other time when I discovered my fears around aging. I found myself once again alone in that many of the women around me were younger, or had hysterectomies, and the whole of literature I discovered was written by male doctors who considered this episode in a woman's life as an affliction best ignored or doused with tranquilizers. Now there are many books written by and for women on this very different change in our lives. At that time I took myself off to a cabin in the country where I lived alone, grew a garden, and had my hot flashes and pseudo-arthritic pains and depressions. Gradually, over a period of years, I adjusted (once again) to yet another process of change in my life.

Self-discovery and personal growth work have been my constant companions, with lots of therapy with wonderful spiritual feminist lesbian workers thrown in. I use the word workers, rather than counselors, because it is all work! This continues where I live now, where I am involved with another women's group — adult children of dysfunctional families (but that is another story).

I am now meeting, through my newsletter and output to various magazines and my writing, some older lesbians. Many have grown up with the knowledge of their lesbianism and some have worked as professionals or in jobs that have not enabled them to be "out" in the world; this can make for a lot of fear about coming out.

There are others who, while recognizing their love for women, are trapped in the so-called security of marriage. However, to all these women who may be afraid of the label of lesbianism and the connotations that society has placed on this word, I would like to say to you that there is joy and strength to be gained in the knowledge of oneself. As we age, why not be as we are meant to be, instead of a reflection of what others desire?

One woman I heard of through SAGE (Senior Action in a Gay Environment coming out of New York), lived alone and was referred to this organization by a social worker after having been in the closet all her life and with a partner. She said, "If I can't come out at the age of ninety-two, when can I?"

The more of us that reveal ourselves, the more society will have to accept our presence. We are a living force to be reckoned with.

SO CRONES, COME OUT, COME OUT, WHEREVER YOU ARE!

Cookie Gant
Mason, Michigan

The One

My name is Cookie Gant. I was born during the 1950s in Detroit, Michigan, at home above the Hastings Bar. Hastings was a main drag street for whores. I was born April 12th in the morning. My mother left me when I was two years old and I never saw her again until my grandmother died. I had no recollection of what this woman looked like, who she was, or anything, and when she walked up to me at my grandmother's funeral and whispered in my ear, "I'm your mother," *I went off!* I just freaked out! When I asked her as I got older why she left she said that my father was abusive. He was never abusive towards me or towards the other kids. I got a bunch of brothers and sisters. I have a bunch over me and I got a bunch under me; twenty-four in all.

I was raised by prostitutes and they took care of me. I mean, they dressed me, they fed me, they gave me money. I was "The One." I don't ever recall any sexual experiences with any of these

This is a transcription of an interview with Cookie Gant, conducted by Terri Jewell.

women, but I always remember them being good to me. My grandmother got real mad at my father because she thought that that was not the environment to bring up a little white girl. My grandmother was half-Indian and half-white. So, my grandmother started raising me. I was five.

The first time that I can remember they noticed that something was different about me was when I was in elementary school. I didn't hear the word "lesbian" or "homosexual," just "different." It had to be somewhere between kindergarten and the second grade. Well, I stole money from my grandmother to buy this girl a camera. You know, one of those little Brownies? I thought she was so pretty. I don't remember her name. My grandmother used to keep five or six of those Crisco cans full of change. I'd just go and help myself and she would never know the damn difference. So, that's how I got the money for the camera. The mother of the girl was so very upset when she found the camera, I got expelled from school for about three days. At first I thought they were expelling me because I stole, but I stole from my grandmother. It was only years later when I recalled the incident that I knew they meant to keep me from this girl. Her parents took the girl out of school. My grandmother would talk to me, but I didn't understand. She said, "Mary's mother is taking her out of school because she's afraid of you." I cried and I said, "Grandmomma, but I love her. I love her and I wouldn't do anything to hurt her." And she said, "Well, baby, you'll understand when you get a little older." I wished the teacher had prevented me from giving it to her instead of Mary taking it home and having her mother freak out.

I had always been called a little tomboy, but after it always came, "She'll grow out of it. She's a tomboy *and* she'll grow out of it." It was after that incident with Mary that I heard "homosexual" applied to myself. My grandmother had died. I was twelve going on thirteen. When my grandmother died, my life stopped, everything ended. I went to stay with my father, and that didn't work out 'cause me and my stepmother couldn't stand each other. When we saw that my stepmother's and my relationship wasn't going to work, my father asked my oldest sister if I could stay with her and he would pick up the tab for me. She is much older than me. She had a marriage of several years, but no children. Her husband was a nut, and abused me. He beat me to the extreme.

My sister put me in Catholic school in Detroit, which I hated. The Visitation School was one entire building going from first to the twelfth grade with only about five blacks at the *most* in the entire school. I was taken out of a black environment that was my life and my foundation, and stuck here with all these white folks. They didn't like me because I'm dark-skinned. And I did not buy into their system, so I was picked on a lot.

There was this girl that came to school named Francine Parrish. I remember her. Francine was a half-breed, tall, and not high-yellow but light skinned. She was so cute. Francine was everything that is feminine. She was not originally from Detroit and was staying with her sister and husband, so we really had a lot in common. When I met Francine, I thought she was the most beautiful thing that walked the face of the earth. I also thought that because she was a half-breed I would have an ally, somebody who I could talk to and walk home from school with. But, I fell in love. I was in the eighth grade.

Falling in love with Francine was my "out." I transferred all that was happening to loving her. I plagiarized Walter Benton's *This is My Beloved* to Francine.

> Yes, your lips match your teats beautifully,
>   rose and rose.
> The hair of your arm's hollow and where your
>   thighs meet
> agree completely, being brown and soft to look at
> like a nest of field mice.
> Praise be the walls that shelter you from eyes that
>   are not mine!

I wrote a lot of letters, six to twelve. I don't know whether her sister accidentally found them, but her family confronted me with a priest. They asked me if I knew that what I was doing was wrong. I said, "Naw. How can my caring for Francine be wrong?" They said, "But some of the things that you've written are very sexual, have sexual overtones." I said, "Well, I got it outta this book! It sounded good to me and I thought it sounded good to her." They asked her, "Francine, what did you do to encourage this?" and "How do you feel about this? Do you want Cookie to continue writing you letters?" They sent her away and expelled me from school. I had to do the rosary three times a day, Hail Marys, and acts of contrition to repent for this great sin that I had committed which I knew nothing about. I had to go to confession and confess. This went on for about a month, maybe longer, and I was so mad because I didn't do anything *wrong*. They wouldn't let me talk to Francine alone. I have a hard time writing people today. It's really hard for me to write my feelings on paper and give them to somebody. I got put out of school for a couple of weeks. I was never so humiliated in all my life. They read it out loud! And they asked me did I know what this meant. I didn't do anything wrong. Why was I being punished? Why were they beating me? What was wrong with calling this girl? "I *love* her!" They just kept on insisting that what I'd done was wrong, that it was a sin.

The first time that I can actually recall having a sexual experience beyond a kiss with a woman was when they committed me to Northfield, an institution that's right outside of Detroit. My stepmother put me in there because she said I was incorrigible. They couldn't prove me "bad," so they proved me "mad." I had just turned fifteen. I was committed September 1, 1964. I got out April 19, 1966. I was seventeen when I got out.

My first lover there was Rosemary Olson, a very fine white girl, whose nickname was Kitten

It is weird when you're institutionalized, because sex is available. It's *there*! I started messing around with Kitten and before I knew it, I had three or four women. They took care of me. They need to condemn that hospital because a lot of people get killed in Northfield. One of my girlfriends got killed and the attendants did it. During these times, a person in a mental institution didn't have any rights, and I was given shock treatments. Kitten and I remained lovers after we both got out of Northfield. I went straight into a Catholic Home, and over half the women that were in there were homosexuals, which made it nice and neat.

My first supposedly "normal" lover after Northfield was Sheba. I didn't know she was a prostitute until after a whole year in a relationship with her. That was a very interesting relationship. She was my lover for three and a half years. She's the only woman who I know that stayed twenty-nine for five years. I said, "Damn, baby, ain't you any older? You were twenty-nine when we first met! And I was eighteen? And you are still twenty-nine? Come on!!" I started having other women and I got really attracted to prostitutes.

Before I entered Northfield, I had identity problems. My father accepted me as I was even when I was a small child. He referred to himself as "Robert Gant and his three sons," which included myself. I had been called a "queer dyke" and a "bulldagger." I had a battle with my religious convictions and my identity as a dyke. For quite awhile, I believed I would die and go to hell for being homosexual. But I was lucky. After Kitten and Northfield, I had a straight woman-friend who accepted me, and kind of adopted me. She would talk to me and let me know that I was okay and wonderful as I was! She would tell me to go inside of myself and love what I found. I am not ashamed of my life. I am strong and mature because of what I have been through. When all else fails, I call on my Higher, Inner Power.

▼

Rhonda Gilliam
Lubbock, Texas

A Journey of Love

Some people feel "coming out" occurs when a person first expresses physical affection for another person of the same sex. Others will tell you "coming out" occurs when a person adopts a gay lifestyle and lives openly within the lesbian and gay community. Still another group will insist that "coming out" involves being completely honest about who you are with family, friends, co-workers, and employers. To me, "coming out" is a process of learning to love and accept myself as I am. By this process of accepting myself, I have been able to exceed the limits placed on me by society. It has been a long journey of love.

Coming out began for me in 1965, at the timid age of fourteen, in a rural Bible-belt town near Lubbock, Texas. I fell in love with my best friend, Sherry. Although the relationship was not sexual, I loved her with all the intensity an adolescent can feel. I dreamed of spending our lives together — loving, sharing, and supporting each other. In my naiveté, I mentioned my love to an older friend. The look of disgust which immediately crossed her face hurt me more than the sternness of her rebuke. I decided to keep my feelings to myself from then on. Soon, Sherry turned away from me and rejected my love, calling it abnormal. I learned from this horrifying experience that I was different, and because of this I felt alone. I felt alienated in a world of uncaring strangers who threatened to be hostile if I tried to be myself. With fourteen-year-old wisdom, I decided to conform. I began to talk about and tried to date boys. I became involved in my church and conformed outwardly to the "normal" behavior that was expected of me. A few months later, I was raped by two boys and stopped dating completely. I spent most of my time outside of school alone in my room, secluded from a world that I thought hated me. I was sure of this because I hated myself. I hated being different. I hated myself for being alone. Even though I had fought with all my strength, I hated myself for not having fought harder to save my dignity from the two boys who raped me. I withdrew into my self-enforced seclusion and dreamed of finding someone who would love me.

During my freshman year in college, I met the first self-acknowledged lesbian I ever knew, Jill, who attended another Texas college across the state. We corresponded by mail until the following summer when she drove to Lubbock to visit me. During that visit, she told me she was a lesbian. At the time, I was heavily involved in Campus Crusade for Christ and believed that she had to renounce her sexuality to become a Christian. During the following fall, we continued to write and often spoke on the phone long distance. I grew very close to her, encouraging and supporting her in the struggle to rid herself of this supposed sin.

I decided to surprise Jill by attending one of her volleyball tournaments near Dallas. When I arrived I sensed that she was uncomfortable. Later that night we were lying on a mattress in a converted attic bedroom and she cried, confessing that she had engaged in casual sex with a woman only the night before my arrival. Through her sobs, Jill told me she would understand it if I hated her. I couldn't bear her pain and her tears tore at my heart. I held her close, trying to console her. As she continued to sob in my arms, her suffering broke through my defenses. It was as simple as kissing away her tears and allowing myself to release the love that I had locked inside myself. When she returned my affection with tender kisses, my heart pounded in a mixture of fear and excitement. Although we didn't have sex that night, we formed a strong bond. Three months later, I turned my back on religion, transferred to her college, and we became lovers.

Loving Jill was the most natural thing I had ever done in my life. I felt completely fulfilled. This feeling was more than sexual desire, it was a sense of belonging, acknowledgement, and most of all, love. I wanted to shout this love from the hilltops, but in 1971 that just wasn't done in East Texas. The few gay friends we had were as closeted as we were. Even private parties were a rarity. We were too young to get into the gay bars in Houston and Dallas, so we kept to ourselves, with only a handful of friends to affirm our love and our right to be together. Against the tide of society's hostility towards lesbians and gay men, we struggled to build our own world of acceptance and love. However, at some point, we began to grow apart. As I grew in confidence and accepted myself as a lovable person, I began to step out of the dark recesses of my closet. I needed freedom. I foolishly tried to gain acceptance through a "straight" woman and lost my first lover in the process.

During my youthful attempts to convince this new woman, Betty, that "gays were okay," I fell in love with her. I loved her ability to be herself. Her carefree attitude and her freedom to do as she pleased attracted me. Yet four months later, when Betty finally fell in love with me, I found she had lost the characteristics that I loved the most. Our relationship was even more restricted than my first one. Betty would not allow me to tell any of my lesbian friends about our relationship. She taught me to play mind games. Through her relentless coaching, I learned to be someone else whenever she wanted me to be, a skill I used countless times, long after our relationship was over.

After I graduated from college, I began to realize the value of this new skill. I started taking pride in my ability to deceive "straight" people. I grew my hair long, wore make-up, and acted like a lady when necessary to avoid the disapproval of my parents, my employers, and my students. My pride in deceiving people took the place of my self-acceptance, and the process of learning to love myself stalled. I had learned Betty's rationalizations well. My job, the acceptance of my co-workers, and my parents' feelings and health became more important than my self-acceptance and self-respect. During the day I wore my disguise and believed in its noble necessity. At night, I sneaked into dimly-lit gay bars to drink away the frustrations and guilt I felt from living a lie. It wasn't until someone important saw through my disguise that I began to learn again to be who I really am.

The person who saw through my charade was a parent of one of the female students on the tennis team I coached. This parent's open rejection of me and my disguise shattered my pride and sent me reeling away in anger. Through a complicated and horrible string of events, aided by my own rebellious anger, this student's mother convinced the principal at my school that I was a lesbian. He explained that my choices were simple — either I resigned or I was fired.

I became despondent. I felt that they had no proof, but I couldn't be sure. If I fought in court and lost, I would lose the teacher's certificate I had gone to college to earn. My name would be spread all over the media and my privacy taken away. Worst of all, my parents would find out. I couldn't take the chance, so I resigned. In seven short months, this woman destroyed the basis for my self-confidence, my closeted identity, and my career. Once again, I was harassed by others for being different. I felt left alone in a void and I was forced to pick up the pieces and find a way to survive.

For the next two years, I struggled to make right the things that had gone wrong in my life. I worked towards being honest with myself as well as other gay people, including prospective lovers. But this honesty didn't extend to the "straight" world because I was still too hurt from the firing to trust them. The process of learning to trust the "straight" world took another six years to accomplish.

During this period, I moved back to Lubbock. Being gay at home was difficult after having lived away for so long. I attended Metropolitan Community Church in Lubbock and the mistrust and uneasiness of my first infrequent visits to the church soon subsided and I continued to open up to others. Eventually, I began to be comfortable in the love I found there and was able to start caring for myself. I came to the realization that God loved me, no matter what my sexual orientation. Although I still had bitter memories of organized religion, I was able to put together the bits and pieces of my personal religion. This discovery added comfort and support in my journey towards loving myself.

One day I was accidentally seen by some "straight" co-workers at Lubbock's newest lesbian bar. I knew everyone at work would know who I was before the week was over. With the support of my friends, I gathered the courage to tell my boss. Though my employer had a non-discriminatory policy that included gays, I was very nervous about telling anyone. The supportive reactions of my co-workers calmed my fears. The feeling of freedom was a high I'll never forget. Soon I became involved in Lubbock's lesbian and gay community and I joined the Lubbock Lesbian/Gay Alliance. I had "come out" in several ways and began feeling better about myself every day, but the biggest hurdle to my sense of freedom remained ahead of me.

I sensed that my parents, who had always loved and supported me, felt hurt by my infrequent, short visits and my inability to share the people who were important to me. In 1983, thirteen years after I had acknowledged that I was a lesbian, I told my parents about my sexual orientation. This revelation was undoubtedly the most frightening experience of my life. Sitting in my parents' living room, I doubted myself and my well-intentioned reasons. My mother's tears and my father's damning silence broke my heart. Yet despite the pain, I felt an inkling of the freedom I needed. As my mother and I worked through our feelings in the coming months, my sense of freedom grew and with it my love for myself flourished.

The process of learning to love myself continues. Sometimes I falter, falling back into lapses of violent anger at the world's unfairness. People's rejection of my lesbianism sometimes hurts me so badly that I want to run away and hide. I often think I might give up except for the love of my friends and my mate, Marcie.

I know that I can survive because I refuse to allow anyone to take away the love and pride I have in myself.

I have spent the last seventeen years on this journey. In the process of learning to love myself, I have loved several women. As I have grown in my love and knowledge of myself, the quality of my relationships has improved. The freedom I feel from society's restrictions has played a large role in this success, and is a direct result of accepting myself for who I am.

▼

Jewelle Gomez
New York, New York

I Lost It at the Movies

My grandmother, Lydia, and my mother, Dolores, were both talking to me from their bathroom stalls in the Times Square movie theatre. I was washing butter from my hands at the sink and didn't think it at all odd. The people in my family are always talking; conversation is a life force in our existence. My great-grandmother, Grace, would narrate her life story from 7 A.M. until we went to bed at night. The only break was when we were reading or the reverential periods when we sat looking out of our tenement windows, observing the neighborhood, which we naturally talked about later.

So it was not odd that Lydia and Dolores talked non-stop from their stalls, oblivious to everyone except us. I hadn't expected it to happen there, though. I hadn't really expected an "it" to happen at all. To be a lesbian was part of who I was, like being left-handed — even when I'd slept with men. When my great-grandmother asked me in the last days of her life if I would be marrying my college boyfriend I said yes, knowing I would not, knowing I was a lesbian.

It seemed a fact that needed no expression. Even my first en-counter with the word "bulldagger" was not charged with emo-tional conflict. As a teen in the 1960s my grandmother told a story about a particular building in our Boston neighborhood that had gone to seed. She described the building's past through the expe-rience of a party she'd attended there thirty years before. The best part of the evening had been a woman she'd met and danced with. Lydia had been a professional dancer and singer on the black theater circuit; to dance with women was who she was. They'd danced, then the woman walked her home and asked her out. I heard the delicacy my grandmother searched for even in her retell-ing of how she'd explained to the "bulldagger," as she called her, that she liked her fine but she was more interested in men. I was struck with how careful my grandmother had been to make it clear to that woman (and in effect to me) that there was no offense taken in her attentions, that she just didn't "go that way," as they used to say. I was so happy at thirteen to have a word for what I knew myself to be. The word was mysterious and curious, as if from a new language that used some other alphabet which left nothing to cling to when touching its curves and crevices. But still a word ex-isted and my grandmother was not flinching in using it. In fact she'd smiled at the good heart and good looks of the bulldagger who'd liked her.

Once I had the knowledge of a word and a sense of its import-ance to me, I didn't feel the need to explain, confess, or define my identity as a lesbian. The process of reclaiming my ethnic identity in this country was already all-consuming. Later, of course, in moments of glorious self-righteousness, I did make declarations. But they were not usually ones I had to make. Mostly they were a testing of the waters. A preparation for the rest of the world which, unlike my grandmother, might not have a grounding in what true love is about. My first lover, the woman who'd been in my bed once a week most of our high school years, finally married. I told her with my poems that I was a lesbian. She was not afraid to ask if what she'd read was about her, about my love for her. So there, amidst her growing children, errant husband, and bowling tro-phies I said yes, the poems were about her and my love for her, a love I'd always regret relinquishing to her reflexive obeisance to tradition. She did not flinch either. We still get drunk together when I go home to Boston.

During the 1970s I focused less on career than on how to eat and be creative at the same time. Graduate school and a string of non-traditional jobs (stage manager, mid-town messenger, etc.) left me so busy I had no time to think about my identity. It was a long time before I made the connection between my desire, my isolation, and the difficulty I had with my writing. I thought of myself as a lesbian between girlfriends — except the between had lasted five years. After some anxiety and frustration I deliberately set about meeting women. Actually, I knew many women, including my closest friend at the time, another black woman also in the theatre. She became uncharacteristically obtuse when I tried to open up and explain my frustration at going to the many parties we attended and being too afraid to approach women I was attracted to, certain I would be rejected either because the women were straight and horrified or gay and terrified of being exposed. For my friend theoretical homosexuality was acceptable, even trendy. Any uncomfortable experience was irrelevant to her. She was impatient and unsympathetic. I drifted away from her in pursuit of the women's community, a phrase that was not in my vocabulary yet, but I knew it was something more than just "women." I fell into that community by connecting with other women writers, and that helped me to focus on my writing and on my social life as a lesbian.

Still, none of my experiences demanded that I bare my soul. I remained honest but not explicit. Expediency, diplomacy, discretion, are all words that come to mind now. At that time I knew no political framework though which to filter my experience. I was more preoccupied with the Attica riots than with Stonewall. The media helped to focus our attentions within a proscribed spectrum and obscure the connections between the issues. I worried about who would shelter Angela Davis, but the concept of sexual politics was remote and theoretical.

I'm not certain exactly when and where the theory and reality converged.

Being a black woman and a lesbian unexpectedly blended like that famous scene in Ingmar Bergman's film *Persona*. The different faces came together as one, and my desire became part of my heritage, my skin, my perspective, my politics, and my future. And I felt sure that it had been my past that helped make the future possible. The women in my family had acted as if their lives were meaningful. Their lives were art. To be a lesbian among them was to be an artist. Perhaps the convergence came when I saw the faces of my great-grandmother, grandmother, and mother in those of the community of women I finally connected with. There was the same adventurous glint in their eyes; the same determined step; the penchant for breaking into song and for not waiting for anyone to take care of them.

I need not pretend to be other than who I was with any of these women. But did I need to declare it? During the holidays when I brought home best friends or lovers my family always welcomed us warmly, clasping us to their magnificent bosoms. Yet there was always an element of silence in our neighborhood, and surprisingly enough in our family, that was disturbing to me. Among the regulars in my father, Duke's, bar, was Maurice. He was eccentric, flamboyant, and still ordinary. He was accorded the same respect by neighborhood children as every other adult. His indiscretions took their place comfortably among the cyclical, Saturday night, man/woman scandals of our neighborhood. I regret never having asked my father how Maurice and he had become friends.

Soon I felt the discomforting silence pressing against my life more persistently. During visits home to Boston it no longer sufficed that Lydia and Dolores were loving and kind to the "friend" I brought home. Maybe it was just my getting older. Living in New York City at the age of thirty in 1980, there was little I kept deliberately hidden from anyone. The genteel silence that hovered around me when I entered our home was palpable but I was unsure whether it was already there when I arrived or if I carried it home within myself. It cut me off from what I knew was a kind of fulfillment available only from my family. The lifeline from Grace, to Lydia, to Dolores, to Jewelle was a strong one. We were bound by so many things, not the least of which was looking so much alike. I was not willing to be orphaned by silence.

If the idea of cathedral weddings and station wagons held no appeal for me, the concept of an extended family was certainly important. But my efforts were stunted by our inability to talk about the life I was creating for myself, for all of us. It felt all the more foolish because I thought I knew how my family would react. I was confident they would respond with their customary aplomb just as they had when I'd first had my hair cut as an Afro (which they hated) or when I brought home friends who were vegetarians (which they found curious). While we had disagreed over some issues, like the fight my mother and I had over Vietnam when I was nineteen, always when the deal went down we sided with each other. Somewhere deep inside I think I believed that neither my grandmother nor my mother would ever censure my choices. Neither had actually raised me; my great-grandmother had done that, and she had been a steely barricade against any encroachment on our personal freedoms and she'd never disapproved out loud of anything I'd done.

But it was not enough to have an unabashed admiration for these women. It is one thing to have pride in how they'd so graciously survived in spite of the odds against them. It was something else to be standing in a Times Square movie theater faced with the chance to say "it" out loud and risk the loss of their brilliant and benevolent smiles.

My mother had started reading the graffitti written on the wall of the bathroom stall. We hooted at each of her dramatic renderings. Then she said (not breaking her rhythm since we all know timing is everything), "Here's one I haven't seen before — 'DYKES UNITE'." There was that profound silence again, as if the frames of my life had ground to a halt. We were in a freeze-frame and options played themselves out in my head in rapid succession: Say nothing? Say something? Say what?

I laughed and said, "Yeah, but have you seen the rubber stamp on my desk at home?"

"No," said my mother with a slight bit of puzzlement. "What does it say?"

"I saw it," my grandmother called out from her stall. "It says: 'Lesbian Money!'"

"What?"

"*Lesbian Money*," Lydia repeated.

"I just stamp it on my big bills," I said tentatively, and we all screamed with laughter. The other woman at the sinks tried to pretend we didn't exist.

Since then there has been little discussion. There have been some moments of awkwardness, usually in social situations where they feel uncertain. Although we have not explored the "it," the shift in our relationship is clear. When I go home it is with my lover and she is received as such. I was lucky. My family was as relieved as I to finally know who I was.

▼

Pamela Gordon
Wells, Maine

English Lessons

I first realized I was different when I was a child. I was always a tomboy and always wanted to play boys' games, like football. I never liked the girls — I thought they were silly with their concerns of boys, dresses, and being good. I never knew what it was that I was feeling, I just knew that I felt different.

In ninth grade, in 1969, I developed a crush on my English teacher, Miss Harrison. All I could think about was impressing her and being a good student. Two years later, in the eleventh grade, I met Miss Eidlitz, another English teacher (years later I ended up earning my M.A. in English!) and I fell head over heels in love with her. I idolized her — I felt everything about her was extra special — her striped turtlenecks, her crew neck sweaters, her ideas, and the way she walked. I had never met anyone quite as wonderful. I took every class she taught and followed her everywhere she went. I knew her complete schedule, where she lived, what kind of car she drove, that she liked to ski and to weave, and that she lived with another English teacher, Miss Thompson. I also remember standing in front of the classroom window, wearing a red shirt that light shone through, so she could see my breasts. I fantasized about her coming into the lockerrooms and seeing me naked. But I was so well socialized to believe in heterosexuality that I never knew I felt any sexual desire towards her.

When I look back, she was obviously a lesbian, but at that time I had no idea. A couple of times Miss Eidlitz asked me if there was something I wanted to talk to her about, but I had no idea what she wanted me to say. So I made up something and said, " I smoke a lot of grass." I was confused. She seemed disgusted at this answer and I was angry that she had asked me this question and then did not like my answer. I discussed the incident with my mother and she also thought it was odd. But now, from the perspective of an older-than-teenage lesbian, I see that Miss Eidlitz must have immediately realized that I was a lesbian and tried, without endangering her job, to talk to me about it.

After my unrequited year of being in love with Miss Eidlitz, I plunged into a sex orgy with men. It puzzled me. Was something in me trying to prove my heterosexuality? Or was I so turned on by Miss Eidlitz that I knew of no other way to satisfy my desires?

That summer of 1971 when I was seventeen, I had my first love affair with a woman. I adored Marlene. She had come into my life as a golfing friend. We got friendlier and friendlier until it seemed all our thoughts and desires were the same. I had very strong feelings for her, but as with Miss Eidlitz, I didn't know what they were. My mom knew what was going on, though, and asked me if Marlene was seducing me. The idea had never occurred to me, but when she brought it up, it sounded like a great idea. I realized then what my attraction was, but Marlene was much older than I was, and married. I didn't believe she could feel anything for me — certainly a married woman couldn't want another woman sexually. But obviously she did desire me, as she wove her web very deftly until I became more and more obsessed with her. I ended up making sexual advances towards her, and kissed her for the first time on the fourteenth fairway. She eagerly accepted my advances, showing me for the first time a woman's wondrous ability to have multiple orgasms.

In the fall, I went to college and labeled my love affair a trial into the exotic and adventurous. I threw myself into my studies, spending almost every waking moment studying or swimming or eating. Suddenly I began to gain weight — I couldn't stop eating. I kept trying to go out with men, but never felt any emotional bonds form with them.

From 1972 until 1982, I virtually eliminated sex from my life. I took a break from college and traveled and worked. Then I finished college and went on to grad school. In the fall of 1982 my mother offered to send me to Duke University's weight loss program. I weighed 199 pounds and my mother was desparate to help me, so off I went.

Not too long after I arrived in North Carolina, I met Laurie — a very large, very in-control, very butch yet oh-so-soft lesbian. I fell head over heels in love with her. I was very upset because I thought my feelings for women were over and done with; had gone away. As I had done before with Miss Eidlitz, I dogged Laurie's every move. We ate together in the dining room and people told me that I sat and gazed lovestruck at her. She and I would go swimming together and I'd swim underwater to see her breasts in the water. We'd play racquetball together and I'd watch her every move. She had a red Chevy van with a loud stereo on which she always played women's music — something I had never heard before. I was so impressed to be with her and so honored whenever I got to ride in her van. Laurie was very political and began talking to me about gay rights and especially about the oppression of women. She opened my eyes to things I'd never seen, let alone imagined. She introduced me to a lot of other dykes and I was amazed at how "normal" they all looked — there was no way you could tell. She took me to women's dances at the local "Y" and to the women's bars, and for the first time, I saw women dancing together, holding each other, kissing. It looked so odd! So different! I felt shocked to see it, yet it *felt* so right. It was a long time before it *looked* right.

For a while, I still had to deny that I could be "one of them." One day I was in Laurie's kitchen with her while she was baking brownies and she said to me, " Face it girl, you are a lesbian. You are turned on by women, you love women."

I said, "No, no that can't be, not me, never." But I began to entertain the idea and I really began to be upset. How could it be?

Me, who had gone to bed with all those men? Me, who hated that awful word "lesbian"? But I kept thinking and watching.

All of this time I had been hot to sleep with Laurie, but she refrained, saying she had a lover back home in Michigan. So when another opportunity presented itself with Carol, who during all my painful trials had been a friend and had loved me, I jumped into bed with her. This time, I knew I truly loved women and that women were for me. I moved in with Carol. Carol was very much in love with me while, truthfully, I only tolerated her. I had been honest from the start, but the relationship began to close in. I moved out and returned to Boston.

It was the fall of 1983 and I had the fervor of a new convert. I threw myself into women's activities, meetings, women's groups, coming out groups, gay causes, gay bars, and lesbians! I read book after book about lesbians and a whole new world opened up to me as I learned how many women are lesbians, how we vary as individuals and how we cope with our lesbianism. I met teenage lesbians, older lesbians, lesbian mothers with children, Jewish lesbians, black lesbians, butch and femme lesbians. I felt I had died and gone to lesbian heaven. I finally fit in somewhere, finally felt totally at home. I no longer felt there was something wrong with me, that I was different — I knew I was different and was relieved to know why. I reveled in seeing so many women who looked like me, not like the traditional feminine women, but women who acted like me and felt like me. Women to learn with, to work out my feelings with. What began to amaze me was how blind and ignorant I had been of my true feelings. I didn't know what the feelings were, all I could say was that I felt strange.

In the summer of 1984 I came out to my mother. I loved her more than anybody else in the world, and I wanted her to know the truth. She wasn't too surprised when I told her that I was not like girls and women were "supposed" to be. She had known all along about all my crushes on my teachers and had heard about all my women friends in North Carolina. Her only worry was that I'd be unhappy — in her eyes how could any woman be happy and survive without a man? She was afraid I would be labeled and hurt all my life because of my choice. She didn't know women could love one another and bond together for life, and she feared I'd be lonely and alone. Then, too, she felt guilty: what had she done wrong to produce a lesbian daughter? Was it her fault? I tried to reassure her about all her fears: that it was nobody's fault, I had been "like this" since birth, that I was happy being a lesbian, that I could find a long-term lover. My mother loved me and accepted me fully and without question, although sometimes she would ask questions about what it was like to sleep with another woman.

My mother and I began having long talks which consisted mostly of me explaining lesbianism to her, sharing my new ideas with her and showing her how I was happy, at peace, and felt I had finally found a home.

My father, on the other hand, hated my lesbianism. He felt he and my mother had failed. He's never forgiven me for what I have "done to him," although he's the one who encouraged me to be a tomboy and act masculine.

I feel neither of my parents should blame themselves. I am what I am and always have been since birth. My lesbianism is a natural expression of my being. I can finally claim the word "lesbian" proudly and joyfully.

I met my lover Barbara one day at the Randolph Country Club, a men's and women's bar near Boston. She walked over to me and asked me if I used to belong to Spring Valley Country Club — her parents had been members there years before. She had watched me play tennis and had developed a crush on me. This common bond spurred us on to talk and soon I felt myself in the magnetic presence of a very special woman. We kissed that night before I left, and I knew I was in love with her. She invited me to come the following night and visit the restaurant she owned. I arrived home from work at 4:00 P.M., showered, picked out my clothes carefully (but before I arrived, had already soaked them with the sweat of my anxiety), and went to visit her. She greeted me with a giant smile and my heart and soul thrilled to be near her. I fell into that smile. I knew that she loved me and that I loved her, and that this was the real thing, yet I didn't dare believe that I had found someone to love. Barbara and I could do little but gaze at each other and into each other's eyes, yet she managed to make me the greatest meatball sub I've ever had.

We are now, two years later, in our own home. We have had lots of good times as well as tough times, weathering sickness and my mother's death. Barbara and I have dealt with her daughter's drug and alcohol problem, poverty, and her parents' moving to Florida — and we are still very much in love. Coming out was the best thing I ever did!

Lisa Gravesen
Goodland, Indiana

Summer Camp

It was April 10, 1971 and I was living in a small Indiana town where no one knew the anguish that had completely overcome me. Even I didn't know why. Why did I have such strong feelings for my fourth grade teacher? I would go to great lengths to capture her undivided attention. She was petite, young and beautiful. I can still recall how upset I was the day she married. Life goes on for a ten-year-old girl, although it wasn't easy.

I knew something was very different about me. All of my girlfriends were developing an interest in boys, but my only interest in them was as companions, to play baseball at the water tower, or fish in the old ice pond. On occassion, I'd even beat them up for calling me names or trying to push me around. Tomboys were not very popular in this small Indiana town.

Donna was my best friend, and just like me. Our parents tried so desperately to keep us apart, but Donna and I were two of a kind. No Barbie dolls for us, thank you! If there was trouble to be found, Donna and I always managed to find it. We couldn't even sit through a Girl Scout meeting without being separated for misbehaving. We always had to laugh and joke around. We were quite the clowns.

In 1973 we went to Camp Sycamore together. It's what every Girl Scout waited for. We paid our ten-cent dues every week for a whole year for this. There were four units at our camp. Each unit had eight tents, and each wooden-floored tent had four cots. Naturally, Donna and I were in the same tent, along with two other girls — Tina and Rose. The first two days were fun, when Donna and I weren't being punished for running away from the other happy campers, or scaring the sissies in the tent next to ours. The third day brought rain. We all sat in the big, two-story cabin singing songs and working on one of the many projects we were required to do. By night, we were all back in our tents telling ghost stories in the storm. We were so frightened we decided to pair up in our cots: Tina and I, Donna and Rose. One thing led to another, and soon we were kissing and exploring each others' young bodies. We fell innocently asleep in each others' arms, safe and secure. To Tina and Rose, it may have been just playing house, but to Donna and I it was so much more; it was the start of a whole new way of life. It was a whole new challenge to conquer.

Camp Sycamore, 1973 ended, but the memories were far from gone. Donna and I played "house" several times after that, but we knew that we weren't lesbians. Lesbians were the two older girls that lived down the street, whom everybody talked about with such disgust. I took quite an interest in these women. I was very curious about the things they did. I couldn't understand why the mere mention of the word "lesbian" left me astounded and eager to learn more. Donna and I didn't talk about these possibilities then; we were taught that being homosexual was a sick sexual perversion, most often categorized with rapists and child molesters. I looked forward with relief to outgrowing this silly phase I was going through.

In 1974 I was thirteen. One dreadful day Donna told me that her family was moving to Elkhart, about three hours away. What would I do without her? I needed her. She had to be the only girl for miles who was as mixed up as I was. I went into a shell. The fear of high school and the fear of being so alone in the small farming community where I grew up were far too much for me to handle. I wanted to run away. I was certain that there were girls in the city who felt like me. How could I possibly fit in with the other girls at school when I had all the interests of a boy? The girls considered me strange, and I knew I was very different from them. While they were making their pretty dresses in home economics and talking about their dates with the jocks, I was building dressers in shop class and excelling in basketball. I tried to be friendly to everyone, but I was not very popular and kept to myself.

I didn't date boys at all. My weekends consisted of shooting baskets and baby sitting. That was how I met Chris. She was nineteen, and I was fifteen. She was married and I would babysit her two little boys. As my feelings for her grew, so did my fantasies. I could no longer lie to myself about my sexuality. As scared as I was, and as much as I hated the word, I realized that I was a lesbian.

Chris was a goddess in my eyes. She was tall, with long dark hair and very prominent cheekbones. She was warm, loving and sensitive. She gave me a sense of security unlike I'd ever felt. Her husband was a salesman, which meant he spent many nights on the road. Chris and I spent hours talking about sex; something I didn't know too much about, but I was more than willing to learn. She was very open minded and I felt at ease discussing any topic with her. When the talks led to my sleeping with another woman, Chris didn't get that terrified look on her face that I was so used to seeing. She seemed curious. I spent many nights with her while her husband was away. It all started out as innocent cuddling, although my intentions were not so innocent. Several times, we were awakened by each other's soft touch, but managed to fight our feelings and go back to sleep. One hot summer night, I very nervously leaned over and gently kissed her lips. She responded. I had been so afraid to lose her friendship. Instead this beautiful woman wanted to make love to me almost as much as I had wanted it to happen. My heart was beating so fast with excitement that I thought I was in heaven. I had never experienced feelings like these, and never knew it was possible to feel so perfectly content. Our secret affair lasted for over a year. They say that the first cut is the deepest and I found this to be true. This woman who meant everything to me was in love with her husband. I wanted her so badly. I couldn't get over her, and I didn't feel I could talk to anyone about it. I couldn't understand why society regarded this most beautiful type of relationship as sick and abnormal.

Hurt, I began to date a man. Dale was a very good-looking man, and really sweet. He was much more gentle than most men I'd come in contact with, and we dated for almost a year — but something was missing. I could not become emotionally attached to him, nor did I enjoy sex with him. I hurt him just as much as Chris hurt me.

After high school, I was introduced to the real world. I met other lesbians, and began to feel very natural about my sexuality. I began working in Monon, Indiana and decided that I would never again need to hide behind an image of what everyone thought I should be. I was very honest with co-workers and invalidated a lot of negative stereotypes that they had of lesbians. To my surprise, they really respected me.

▼

Gillian Hanscombe
Devon, England

Sweating, Thumping, Telling

I'm sitting at a double-desk (replete with two removable, white porcelain inkwells being filled from a large bottle by the ink monitor) second to the back row, in an Australian State School classroom. It's 1952 and I'm seven years old. Diagonally behind me sits Glenys Hill, who taps me on the shoulder, wanting to borrow a pencil. I turn around. With what I later learn from books is a thumping heart, I think in words, "I love Glenys Hill!"

Then I'm nine, walking round the back of the girls' shelter-shed where we eat packed lunches, arm-in-arm with Terrie Fisher. I say to her "I love you." She says, "Do you mean like a man loves a woman?" Oh yes, I'm about to say, oh yes. But she goes on, "Or like a friend loves a friend?" I say "yes" to that, knowing nothing, but somehow knowing this second yes is the correct yes.

Next I'm twelve. I've gone to a fee-paying girls' school run by Church of England nuns, where my mother had been a boarder thirty years before. I'm entranced by a bigger girl deigning to talk to me. She's called Maxine and is frightfully strong. She's fourteen and hits tennis balls harder than anyone in the school. She teaches me to hit tennis balls too, every morning before school (I get up at seven to be there for as long as possible) and every afternoon (my mother rages when I'm not home until eight at night). Our fingers touch as we sway about standing squashed together in the athletics team bus. I sweat and thump like anything. She writes me hugely long letters, hugely long poems in the style of Tennyson, Milton, and the Shakespeare of the History plays, though I won't know the originals until much later. We "wrestle" in the cloakrooms. She calls it wrestling and she always wins, but I don't mind a bit being pinned down by her. "I love you," she says fiercely against my sweating ear, my burning head held hard down flat on the concrete. The other girls snigger when they catch us but I'm only dimly aware that they don't do these things.

It's the holidays. I spend a week at Maxine's house. Both her parents go to work so we're alone. We spend all day in bed, hugging and kissing, declaring passion, kissing some more. We don't take our clothes off and don't know what else to do, other than kissing and hugging.

After a year, my mother confronts me. She's found my shoeboxes stuffed with Maxine's letters and poems. She burns them all. She's worried about me. On the advice of the family doctor, a woman, my mother makes me join a mixed church fellowship and a mixed dancing class. I get crushes on the young woman who runs the church fellowship and on one of the girls at the dancing class, but I don't tell anyone. I kiss all the boys who want to kiss me but my heart never thumps. I only care that one or other of them kisses me so I can pass with the other girls.

I fall in love with God for a while, and then with my English teacher, who's twenty-two. I'm fifteen and she spends time with me out of school, telling me about modern poetry and herself. We hug and kiss a lot but she won't let me take her clothes off. I vaguely want to, though. My father thinks this friendship "unhealthy" and gets my mother to send me to see the doctor again. The doctor prescribes more "mixed" activities and activity generally.

Then I'm sixteen and in my last year of school. My heart thumps again. She's called Patsie and is a boarder at a different school. We've met on and off for years when our schools have played each other at tennis, softball, basketball, and so on. We make friends and write letters. She spends a boarders' weekend with me. I stay at her house in the holidays and we lie in bed together, declaring love and passion. One night she says, "I don't think either of us has any inhibitions," and slips her hand down my pyjama waist, down my belly, down to my pubic hair. I do the same to her. I wonder what all the sticky wet is, having no idea. We rub a lot...

Her mother phones my mother. She's opened a letter I posted to Patsie. She says to my mother, "I've never *seen* such a letter in my life. I would never write such a letter to my own husband." "And she has five children," my mother explains to me, dreadfully distressed. I can't make it out. My letter has words in it like breasts and hair and thighs. Wanting them, that is. Wanting Patsie. Don't wives want their husbands, then? Patsie's mother doesn't seem to. My mother doesn't seem to, either. Women don't??

I'm sent to another doctor. She says it will all pass. She says I should meet more boys. I've already met all the boys the other girls have met. "Meet more then," she says heartily.

Later I'm sent for psychoanalysis. I do that for four years and it makes me better and stronger and saner. During that time I have Kerryn and Ruth and Kate and others ... By now I know the word lesbian (it's in the books) and the word orgasm (it's in the same books) and I've had sex with men but it never once made my heart thump.

I'm twenty-three and living with a lover called D. We plan to go to Europe and live in England for a bit. She's a musician. I want to travel and write, but what I really want to do is get away with being a lesbian. A couple of years later, on a visit back home, I talk to my mother. She worries all the time about me being "alone" and "not settled" in England. "I'm not alone," I tell her. "If you're going to worry, it may as well be about something true rather than something not true. D is my lover. We live together and sleep together. I'm a lesbian. I'm not alone."

My mother mourns. She's a Christian and thinks it's wrong and that she's wrong and what did she do wrong? "Nothing," I tell her, but it's no use. She mourns and worries and blames herself. But she doesn't change towards me.

Three years later, my mother dies suddenly. I plan to have a baby and become pregnant. I lose that baby and try again, this time successfully. I learn about feminism and gay liberation. I join things, start writing differently, and feel better and better about being lesbian. But I'm not too sure I can pinpoint my coming out. If you live like a lesbian before you know the word, it all just feels like going on and growing up.

▼

Linda Heal
Madison, Wisconsin

A Flower Box

Only a week before, we had done our first loads of laundry together at college. Carefully following my mom's written instructions, we separated the whites and colors, and then, at fifty cents per load, decided to consolidate everything into one machine — we'd deal with laundry that didn't win awards.

We were eighteen and freshmen at a small liberal arts college in an Illinois town of about 100,000. It was September of 1983 and the first class I went to was Social Problems, where I sat behind a quietly intense woman in beat-up running shoes. Being an ex-jock, I'm always looking at the quality of people's footwear to see how seriously they take themselves. That person turned out to be Kay, and on an October evening we decided to get together to study for our college exam premiere in Social Problems.

We opted to study while walking on Main Street — Kay was constantly in motion, so this studying on foot wasn't uncharacteristic. We had barely touched the material in Section One when she sat down in a flower box in front of a tan spa and perched on its edge.

"Can I trust you?" she said. "And can you trust me?" I nodded to both of these and I heard in the rhythm of Kay's voice that if the pacing of her questions slowed she would never get her words out. "Are you gay or straight? Me, I'm as queer as a three-dollar bill."

And there it was in a chill over Main Street — the question I'd avoided thinking about for the past five years. But there was something new, a good reason to say, "Yeah. Maybe," to a supportive person asking it. So I said it. "Yeah, maybe. I mean, I've always thought I probably was, but I've never had the opportunity. I've never checked it out." And I hadn't. I grew up in a midwestern town of 14,000 that acted even smaller. Openly gay men and women were as hard to find as tasteful radio stations, so I was stuck without role models, or even accepting people to talk with about what I thought was happening with me. Once when I was fourteen and tried to bring it up with Mom, all I could say was, "Mom, the other kids are calling me gay." I choked on what I wanted to say next — "And I think they're right."

I first realized there was such a thing as homosexuality when I was eleven and watching the previews for the next week's episode of *Family*. One of Willie's friends had come out to him, and then they cut to the preview scene where mother Kate talks to daughter Buddy — "Do you know what a homosexual is, Buddy?"

"Yeah. A guy who likes a guy or a girl who likes a girl."

The preview didn't open any doors for me — in fact, by the next week when the actual episode was on, I had to ask at the first commercial break what homosexuality was. But after that, I remembered.

I had just turned thirteen when I noticed my attachments to my new female friends seemed somehow different, kind of romantic. I hesitantly admitted it a year later in my journal, about fifteen pages after I talked about how close I felt to Michelle and Julie, how much I respected them because they ignored the other kids who kept asking me if I was going to have a husband or a wife, or if Renee Richards was my hero. I knew that my love surpassed ordinary love and respect — I just knew that nobody felt as passionate about members of their own gender as I felt about Julie and Michelle.

"I think I'm gay," I wrote in my early teen handwriting that vascillated between the large loopy way everybody else wrote and my own tight pointy letters. "It isn't from other people calling me that — I just have what adults would call 'very confusing feelings.' Damn right they're confusing. I'm not attracted to boys at all. I want to be with Julie and I want to do with her the things I'm supposed to want to do with boys. Damn it, what's going on? I think I love her. What's the matter with me?"

Clearly I was different from the other eighth graders and my peers had noticed I could live with being different because I came with an intact sense of self-esteem. When people ask me what role my family played in my lesbianism, I tell them, "They encouraged me to feel self-esteem, even though I didn't yet know I was a lesbian, so that I could face up to who I was and wouldn't stifle myself by pretending I'm something I'm obviously not." Because of this self-esteem and a good sense of humor I was accepted, even if I was "the weird one."

Despite my feeling comfortable much of the time in the face of being called "weird," this feeling of weirdness and knowing that I was a lesbian also frightened me. It frightened me so much I went into hiding for four years. I never acted on my feelings for women, hoping that eventually they'd evolve into heterosexual feelings. I could even be spotted at high school dances, being a good sport about the death by pantyhose I was suffering underneath the long dresses I wore at those events.

All the while I knew that I was shushing a chunky part of myself, and that hurt. I stopped writing journals because introspection was dangerous. I stopped reading, because I never knew when a teenage character would strike some nerve and I'd get upset. I poured myself into being busy — I played volleyball, basketball, softball, wrote the yearbook, and fell in love with early American literature, which seemed safely removed, reading these stories that never talked about love, only solitary men freezing to death on tundras.

All that squelching had brought me here, to a flower box on Main Street where I finally decided that what I had been ignoring might have some positive force.

Kay and I kept walking and talking and I was finally able to share my confusion and the pain of hiding with someone who knew what it was all about. I could ask somebody else the questions I'd been stewing about. It was Kay, for instance, who made me realize that maybe it just doesn't matter how we got to be gay in the first place. "That's all history," she said. "What we need to deal with is now. We can choose to accept the fact that things work out differently for us than for most people. Or we can choose to ignore it."

I had tried ignoring it, and that was extremely uncomfortable. Now, I was one hundred miles away from my hometown, family, and all the people that would hold me to my past, and was more than ready for a clean start.

Kay told me that she found me attractive and, if I wouldn't feel too crowded, perhaps we could start seeing each other romantically. On Main Street, we started what was to be a sixteen-month relationship.

At first there were a lot of secretive smiles — it felt like a secret affair, and the sparks I felt with Kay were something new, coming so easily and naturally after all those high school years when I had tried to convince myself that I felt there was some sort of fleshy interest in the guy I was dating. When we slept together three weeks later lovemaking came very easily. There was an undeniable feeling in my flesh that this was how things are best for me, that I was meant to love a woman's softness.

Coming out to myself, as much as it was a relief, was still a stressful time for me. My roommate, a petite prom queen with a tiny squeaky voice, found out that Kay and I were more than friends. She freaked out and moved out — evidence that I was now a social nasty. I noticed an increasing distance when I talked with Mom; every time I picked up the phone I tried to become who I'd been in high school and the fast transitions between the two worlds made my ears ring.

When things got tough for me, I remembered that it was even more uncomfortable denying who I was. It seemed I'd been given my choice of pains, and I chose to face the pains that would move me closer to being a strong person. Although I'd been in hiding for four years, the distress had never abated. After coming out, my dealings with other people's nonacceptance could at least be balanced with self-esteem.

As I became more and more comfortable with myself and

other gay students through the gay student support group at a nearby larger university, I realized that I needed to let Mom know. We've always had a close relationship and she was good at not meddling and at letting me try the things I needed to do. Mom's laissez-faire attitude allowed me to take a lot of responsibility and earned my respect for her because she trusted me as much as she did. I thought Mom would want to know that I was in love for the first time. As insightful as Mom is, I thought she probably already knew that I had lesbian leanings, I told myself as I headed downstairs one weekend to help her with the dishes.

To my surprise, telling her caught her completely off-balance, as though just moments before she'd been planning to talk to me about birth-control methods. She hadn't made anything of my lack of kinship with the high school guys I'd dated, and hadn't made any assumptions about my intense connections with my women friends. Either my heterosexual facade had been too convincing, or Mom, like me, had worked at ignoring many things.

Mom finally believed me when she realized I intended to live as a lesbian, and she went through a lot of blaming. First she blamed Kay, saying, "Maybe you just want the bond of her friendship so much you'll do whatever she tells you to — even act like a lover." When I reiterated that I'd had these feelings for women long before I met Kay, Mom started blaming herself. She said, "I guess Dad and I don't show enough affection for each other in front of you, and you haven't seen how strong male-female love can be."

Mom's insistence on seeing things this way put a new strain on our relationship. I felt that she was knocking my strength as a human — how *dare* she assert that I was weak enough to be made into a puppet by anyone, including Kay. Further, I felt that she was ignoring my ability to love, something she'd nurtured in me. I had trusted my mother to trust my judgment, and she'd let me down for the first time. I didn't want my relationship with Mom to get stuck at that point, but I knew that I wouldn't break things off with Kay in an attempt to fix things with Mom.

Mom and I had constant dialogue when I was home over weekends. We had to look through our hurts and make efforts to know what the other was feeling. Mom needed to see that I was the same person, that I wasn't rebelling against every value that she'd ever taught me, but taking that value scheme with me into my lesbian life. She needed to see that being a lesbian was a whole way of loving, not just a string of sexual encounters. I had to try not to be too hurt when she insinuated that perhaps this was just a phase, that I could change. And I had to consider that her sudden disorientation sometimes colored our talks differently and I had to remember to be gentle with her when I wanted to be indignant or self-righteous. Our efforts to be understanding went both ways, and Mom started to accept me, while I learned to be patient, and thrilled with her gradual progression.

The longevity of my relationship with Kay convinced Mom that I was sure about what I was doing. As my sixteen-month relationship with Kay progressed Mom made genuine efforts to like her and began trying to get used to the idea that we were happy together.

In the two years since my relationship with Kay ended, Mom has made tremendous strides and now accepts me. This makes me the envy of my gay friends, who are all in some stage of dealing with, or not dealing with, their parents. Mom is ready to donate some positive books to our high school library, because there's nothing there about homosexuality, and there are some kids who really need to read about what they're going through. Mom has met all my favorite lesbian friends and has genuinely enjoyed the women I love.

My father, my younger brother and sister, and Mom's parents all know now, and I think it was Mom's patient acceptance that kept them from saying, "Ewww, gross" when she told them. My grandparents kept hoping for a change, but now, three years later, they make it even clearer that they love me. My brother and sister were twelve and fourteen when they found out — an age when being "different" isn't always welcome. Since that age was their own time of stumbling into sexual awareness, my lesbianism isn't something we talk about too much. But since they're sensitive and we all really enjoy each other, I think they see that gay people aren't only the lisping queen stereotypes that show up in homophobic jokes.

Things have worked out extremely well for me, despite an understandably rough start. I feel so much more genuine for having accepted my lesbianism and having integrated that acceptance into my family relationships. All the coming-out scrapes and bruises seem a bargain to me now. I know how it feels to have my sexuality in the open, and how it feels to enjoy the acceptance of the people I love the most — including myself.

Sarah Holmes
Boston, Massachusetts

Groundworks

Even before I came out, I often felt I was a lesbian. I resolved that question when I was twenty-six, living in Boston and active in the feminist movement. In the seven years since then, I keep discovering new facets of being lesbian and it seems as coming out is something that never ends, it just evolves. Although there was that intense moment of recognition, when I said, "Yes, this is who I am," coming out is about continually uncovering and affirming feelings and connections with women. I come out every time I hold an open conversation about my life in a public place, read a lesbian book or newspaper on the subway, or speak publicly on a lesbian or gay issue. Although now I'm out to almost everybody in my life, there are always situations where I question whether to explain who I am, or "pass."

Growing up having close and also physical relationships with girls made me feel different. When I was a child I told my mother repeatedly that I was never going to get married, and I was very stubborn about it. I was never able to envision myself in that kind of a relationship with a man; the idea of being married always seemed alien.

I explored sex before most kids in my neighborhood did, and I had a very sexual relationship with a girlfriend of mine that started when I was seven and continued for many years. We lived in a midwestern city, and would spend Saturday nights sleeping over at each other's houses before being delivered back to our respective families the next Sunday morning at church. We were eager to go to bed, seldom arguing to stay up late to watch TV. We would go into the bedroom and stay up all night playing in bed, with candles or a low light burning. Once we were caught when I put my pink bathrobe over the lamp to create a warm erotic glow and the lamp caught the robe on fire.

That quelled things for a while because we were worried that our parents would wonder what two nine-year-old girls would do in the middle of the night with no pajamas on.

We played witches mostly, taking turns being good and bad, making each other do pleasurable and mean things to each other. We traveled over each other's bodies, and through each other's minds and fantasies for years this way, and when we didn't see each other as much because I moved to Madison, I came away knowing that it was possible to have that kind of physical intimacy with another girl. I found out from a babysitter what grown-ups did to make babies. She said that they got on top of one another and rubbed their private parts together. That was what Jodie and I did, and it didn't make sense to me that I had to be with a boy to do that.

I carried a strong sense that I was different through adolescence. I knew I could be happy just being with my girlfriends and boys seemed unneccessary, even bothersome. I had a boyfriend in sixth grade, until I broke up with him when I found out that he had a lot of set ideas on what I was supposed to do just because I was his girlfriend, like going to football games and giving him Donovan records. I didn't like that and after I broke up with him I was done with being involved with boys for a long time. I had a few crushes on boys, but generally they all bored me, and I preferred writing intense notes back and forth with my girlfriends, and talking for hours on the phone after school to being part of the boy-girl chase.

When I was fourteen I fell in love with my best friend and

began to wonder if I was a lesbian. I had read about lesbians in Mary McCarthy's *The Group*. I wanted to spend all of my time with her, and I dropped several friends because they paled beside the excitement that I felt when I was with her. When we walked down State Street after school browsing in bookstores, spent hours listening to Joan Baez or Arlo Guthrie records, danced to Beatles records, planned our lives and shared everything we knew, I felt more in tune with her than I had ever felt with anybody. When we walked together through the halls of school or on the way home, sharing secrets, I felt like our bodies were in complete synchronization.

She was my best friend even after I moved away to Albany, New York and I spent much of high school writing her letters, single-spaced typewritten letters seventeen pages long. I lived with a passion for her return letters. When I would come home from school and find one of her thick letters in a long envelope with her artistic handwriting on it, I would run upstairs until dinner, not wanting to be with anybody but her. I yearned for those vacations when I was able to go back to Madison to see her, or she would come east and we could spend time in person. I didn't date, but spent a lot of time with a youth group and worked a lot on political campaigns, and my emotional life centered on her and other women friends.

When I went to college in Massachusetts in 1973, I began to take women's studies courses during my first year. A friend commented that the only thing I seemed truly excited about studying was women. I went to spend that summer in Albany and took an intensive women's studies course that met every morning. Every afternoon I wrote pages in my journal and read all the books and articles on the "more than required reading" list. I encountered many out lesbians from Albany in that class, older women in their late twenties and thirties, many taking this course when the lesbian community was just beginning to surface in Albany and find each other. We talked openly about sexuality, homophobia, and conflicts between lesbians and straight women. The professor was a lesbian who was very outspoken about the pain of having been closeted.

I became very caught up in the class and got a crush on one of the other women. When I returned to college that fall, I announced to my friends that I had a crush on a lesbian and was bisexual.

When I was twenty-one I took a year off from college and moved to Boston, where I became involved with my first male lover. One of the major reasons why I was drawn to him was that he knew about and supported my bisexuality, which strengthened our bond. I knew I was going to have women lovers at some time before my life was over. I thought a lot about ways of being involved with both women and men, emotionally and sexually, and differences in relationships with people of different genders.

In Boston the lesbian and feminist community was thriving and reading, thinking, and talking a lot about feminism and sex roles. In 1978 I went to my first Gay Pride march in Boston because I was interested to see what it was like and I felt proud and excited to be there. I wondered if people thought I was a lesbian, even though I was there with a man, and felt pleased by that prospect.

Being bisexual, with women as close friends but sleeping with men, changed after I broke up with my last male lover in 1979. I was still bisexual for a couple of years, but any desire to be involved with men soon abated. I had an affair with a good friend from the Women's Center and fell in love with her, although she moved away from Boston. We spent hours staring at each other in meetings, hours leafletting dark streets for the feminist campaign we worked on, and hours in bed and on my living room sofa, drinking white wine and arguing about separatism and whether you could exist in this world without men. Those discussions were an integral part of my coming out as a lesbian. Having sex with her was very easy and natural, I felt *loving* towards her in a way I had not with men.

I still considered myself bisexual, until one Saturday afternoon in 1981 at a feminist forum at a university in Boston. Everything that had been building within for years, growing towards coming out, rushed to a head that day. I looked deeply into the eyes of a woman I had long admired, a lesbian activist in her midthirties that I knew through my political work. I knew for sure that I was a lesbian and that she knew too. I looked closely at her a second time, feeling another wave of recognition and mutual interest, and again a third time for a long, slow stare full of energy and desire. Then, I looked shyly away, until finally I looked a fourth time with a sense of firm connection, knowing that *yes, we are in this life together.* She never became my lover, and in fact, what I had felt standing before her was so intense I felt awkward around her for a long time after that. The years of questioning and the simmering consciousness that I was a lesbian erupted in me in that moment when I knew there was no going back. She became a role model for me. I was fascinated by the sight of her and by being in the same room with her, every detail about her was etched with a significance I had not felt before. I felt more excitement and energy for life than I had felt before coming out. I would think about her all the time, in meetings, at work, in conjunction with books I was reading. I would think of her whenever I had an interesting perception or observation. She was not the only woman on my mind those days, but she was the beacon and in my head and heart the most.

After I came out, I became much more aware of homophobia. I had always sensed it in others, and in myself, although I didn't always have the word to describe it. My images of lesbians during high school and college were positive — compelling, appealing, and romantic, but I felt scared to go towards other lesbians. I sensed that lesbian relationships weren't approved of, and my images of lesbians contrasted with the admonitions I received from my parents when I didn't act "feminine" enough, which was often. I was never the lady I was raised to be. When I grew older and read feminist literature and *Gay Community News*, I began to know well the slights, oppression and discrimination that lesbians experience. This knowledge didn't make it easier to come out, although those same books and newspapers offered me an essential connection to the community. Holding out the possibility of getting involved with a man gave me a cushion of heterosexual privilege which I wasn't ready to give up. I didn't know how my parents or old friends would take the news, or the possible discriminations I would face. But as time went on, describing myself as bisexual felt more and more inauthentic, and it became clear to me that I was more strongly committed and connected to women.

Coming out also brought me closer to a feeling of community than I had ever felt before, yet at the same time I felt more alienated from the mainstream world. I felt what I was experiencing was so intensely personal (although I was fully aware of the political aspects of being a lesbian), that I wanted time within myself and with close friends and lovers to explore my passions for women. Every day during my lunch hour and over weekends I hungrily read lesbian/feminist and gay literature, Adrienne Rich, Marilyn Frye, and every book that Persephone Press ever published. Those years were socially very separatist for me. My social and political life revolved around women, lesbians, but I also kept up a number of important friendships with straight or bisexual women, and a couple of male friends from college or a collective house I had lived in. I felt a great deal of sureness and relief in coming out, and felt like I could do almost anything. Being closeted to my parents and at work was hard, and I felt the contradictions between straight people's assumptions of who I was and my own knowledge and sense of myself; but the joy, power and rightness I felt in coming out has made it worth the long process.

Marcie Just
Glenwood Springs, Colorado

Sharp-Shooter

Another school year was begin-
ning and with it the transfer to senior high. It was 1965 in East St.
Louis and my primary concerns were thoughts of teachers, class-
mates, and new friends. I was making my first attempt at learning
a foreign language, and had chosen Spanish.

Spanish class was only a short stroll down the hall from my
home room, so I was one of the first to arrive. I took a seat at the
back of the classroom so I could check out the others as they arrived. All the faces were new, but one in particular caught my eye.
There was something about her. I noted how well her dark blue
sweater contrasted with her brown hair. My eyes followed her as
she took a seat close to mine.

Soon the teacher arrived and called the class to order. "I am
Miss Santos," she informed us. She took the seat behind her desk.
"As I call each of your names, please tell something about
yourself." She glanced at the list of students. "Barbara Andrews,"
she called, and looked out at the class. The girl who had caught my
eye raised her hand.

"I'm a junior and assistant captain of the cheerleading squad,"
she said proudly in a musical voice.

I found it hard to concentrate on the others and kept glancing at Barbara and wondering what she was like. When my name was called I raised my hand. Barbara looked around, and our eyes met. All thoughts were driven from my mind. After what seemed like a long time, I managed to bring my thoughts under control. "I'm a sophomore," I stammered.

Miss Santos smiled. "I don't often have sophmores in my classes," she said. "Why did you decide to take it this year?"

"I've wanted to study Spanish since I was in sixth grade, so I decided to take it as soon as I could," I answered. Miss Santos smiled again, then glanced down at her list.

I looked again at Barbara and found her smiling at me. I smiled back, then looked away before anyone else could notice. My heart was beating faster. I wanted to sing! But I also felt confused. I had been told that feelings like these were what I would feel for a man. I quickly decided I should put Barbara out of my mind and not give her another thought.

Gym was my last class of the day and I welcomed the break from academia. I was sitting on the last step of the bleachers watching the class assemble, when Barbara walked in carrying her orange-and-blue pom poms. She glanced about and saw me sitting there. She waved at me, smiled, and then made her way to the locker room.

A woman sitting next to me asked, "Do you know her?"

"She's in my Spanish class," I said, trying to sound casual.

"The cheerleaders practice during the last hour," she said, answering my unspoken question.

Barbara would be in the locker room at the same time as I was. That thought made the strange feelings return. I tried to shove thoughts of her aside but I kept seeing her face in my mind.

As the term progressed, I found myself waiting impatiently for Spanish class, so I could hear her voice as she recited. Then I couldn't wait for gym class. Occassionally, while dressing for gym, I would catch a glimpse of her bare shoulder, just before she slipped into her cheerleader sweater, or see her dressed only in bra and panties as she changed back to her street clothes. As I finished dressing I would imagine caressing her and feeling her softness and warmth. I wanted to run my hands through her short brown hair, and hear her speak my name. During this very turbulent and emotional time I learned a name for what I was.

A new neighbor had moved in across the street. She wasn't like most of the women in the neighborhood. I watched her for a while, trying to figure her out. The neighborhood women wore dresses and were usually shepherding children. She always wore slacks, men's shirts, and work boots. She was often alone, and seemed to keep to herself. I imagined she must be lonely.

One day I decided to go over and introduce myself. I felt a bit timid as I knocked on her door, not knowing how she would react to my being there. As I waited for her to answer, it occurred to me that maybe she liked being alone. As I thought of going back home, she came to the door. She opened it wide and stepped out onto the porch. I had to look up to meet her eyes, and felt relief that they held welcome.

"I'm a neighbor," I said. "I live in the white house across the street."

She looked across the street and nodded. Her gaze turned back to me.

"I'm Nora," she said, extending her hand.

"Marcie," I said as I shook it.

"Would you like to come in?" she asked.

I nodded.

She closed the door behind us. "Have a seat," she said, motioning towards the flowered couch. "Can I get you a soda?"

"Yes, ma'am. I'd like that," I answered.

As she walked toward her kitchen, I realized how ridiculous her large body would look in the kind of dresses the women in the neighborhood wore. Besides, she seemed comfortable dressing the way she did.

She returned with the soda, handed it to me, then seated herself in one of the chairs.

"Are you in high school? You look about that age," she said.

"I'm a sophomore," I replied, and took a drink of the soda.

She nodded, "I guess you'd like to know something about me," she said half amused.

"I admit I'm curious," I answered.

"I was a nurse during the Korean War, and then chose to pursue a career in the army," she explained. "I retired recently and decided to come back home."

Momentarily there was a look in her eyes that I couldn't understand, but she continued her story before I could think about it.

"When I went to East Saint Louis Senior High, it was a small building downtown. Nothing like the nice school you go to."

We were quiet for a moment, then she said, "I'd like to show you something. I'll be right back."

She returned with what appeared to be a picture frame. She sat next to me on the couch.

"These are my sharp-shooter medals," she said proudly. "That one," she said, pointing to a minature rifle, "I won when I out-shot every man on the field."

"Wow, are you still that good?" I asked.

"I got a five-point buck last winter," she boasted.

I didn't know what a five-point buck was, but she was proud of it. I smiled broadly.

"The other medals aren't very impressive," she said. She set them aside. "Now tell me about you." Her brown eyes showed genuine interest.

"I'm the fifth oldest of ten children, and the oldest one at home now. My interests range from reading and playing guitar to coaching a softball team. I like to play volleyball, too."

Then she asked the question I dreaded most. "Do you have a boyfriend?"

"No," I answered honestly. "Most of the guys want to talk about cars, and frankly, I'm not interested."

To my surprise, she smiled, and nodded as if she had already figured I didn't.

Thoughts of Barbara came to mind, and I suddenly wanted to run, before she could know what I was thinking. I stood and said, "Nora, I have to go now and help Mom with dinner, but I'll be back."

Her eyes held mine with a measuring stare, but she didn't try to stop me.

"Come anytime. I've enjoyed our talk."

"Thanks for the soda," I said as she saw me to the door. I almost ran home. Somehow Nora seemed to know something about me and I wasn't entirely comfortable with that thought.

I rushed into the house and found my mother in the kitchen. Standing in the doorway, I told her about Nora.

"Mom, I met our new neighbor. Her name is Nora. She is a retired army nurse, and has sharp-shooter medals too. Nora got a five-point buck last winter." I said all in one breath.

Mother gave a look of warning, and glanced in the direction of the living room.

In my enthusiam to share my information about Nora, I had rushed by without seeing my father.

He made a disaproving sound, and rustled the newspaper. "Hunting is not for women," he said gruffly. "The mannish bitch ought to get herself a husband." The newspaper rustled again.

I turned to make a comment, and felt my mother's restraining grip on my arm. "Will you peel the potatoes?" she asked gently.

Before I had the chance to talk with Nora again I discovered something about her. Nora had a lady friend. At least once a week, her bright green Chevrolet was parked in front of Nora's house. My first impression of her was that she must be a professional of some sort, as she usually wore skirts and matching jackets

I looked forward to seeing Nora after her friend had visited. She always seemed so happy. The sadness in her eyes, that I believed must have come from being a nurse during the Korean war, would be replaced with joy. We never spoke of the other woman, so I never learned her name, or anything about her.

One evening, when my father came from work, I could tell by the noise he was making that he was in a bad mood. I wished in vain that I was upstairs safely in my bedroom, but unfortunately I was in the kitchen. I braced myself as he stormed into the room. He headed for the refrigerator and got a beer. He took a long swallow, then sighed. By the way he stood I knew he was mad about something. I glanced over at my mother. She was drying her hands on a towel. "Supper will be ready soon, dear. Why don't you read the paper, while you wait, " she said soothingly.

He took another drink, then crushed the can.

"You never see her with a man," he said. "And she's always dressed like one." His contempt was plain in the tone of his voice. "Mannish bitch."

I didn't have to ask who he meant, and Mother's silence seemed to indicate she knew as well.

"Every time you turn around that blonde bitch is over there. I wonder what those queers do in bed," he said contemptuously as he turned and left the kitchen.

"I'll be right back," I told my mother, and went upstairs to my room. My thoughts raced as I sat there hearing his words repeat in my mind. I wanted to talk to Nora. I wanted to know if she felt for the blonde lady what I felt for Barbara.

At dinner my father was still in a sullen mood. I kept my eyes on my plate and desperately tried to avoid calling his attention to me. Just when I thought we'd get through dinner without a tirade, he dropped the bombshell. "Marcie, I don't want you to go over there," he said in a tone that indicated no argument was possible. "I don't want you near that queer, again. Is that understood?"

I lifted my eyes to look at him as I answered, "Yes, sir." A look of hatred was in his eyes. I never visited Nora again, nor did I find anyone during high school to share my feelings with.

In college the game seemed to accept more diversity in its players and amidst this freedom I found courage.

I met her in the fall of 1970, during my junior year at Southern Illinois University. I was in the cafeteria of the student union, struggling over the material for a quiz in geography.

Mary Lou flipped into the chair across from me. "Another map quiz?" she asked solititously.

"Yeah," I said and looked up. Next to Mary Lou sat a woman wrapped in a green cape. Her long blonde hair cascaded over it. She leaned over the table and looked curiously at the map for a moment.

Mary Lou chose that moment to introduce us. "Louise, this is Marcie," she said, and we all turned quickly back to the map.

Louise was a whiz. She made sense out of squiggles that were rivers. Lakes, forests, and mountains were clearly visible to her eyes. I was impressed.

She was not what others would call beautiful. She was short

and round, and had a square, heavy-featured face. But I saw a beauty and power in her that strongly attracted me.

We talked often after that and discovered our mutual love of music and sports. Her blue eyes would sparkle as we discussed the exploits of our favorite hockey player. That winter her parents took a ski vacation, and she invited me to stay with her while they were gone. The house sat apart from the others on the lane, at the edge of a forest. The tranquil setting soon worked its magic and we began to relax.

Late one afternoon, after our classes, we came to the house. I put an album on the turntable as she prepared dinner. I built a fire, and sat down in front of it. Shortly she joined me. "Dinner won't need my attention for a while," she said, making herself comfortable next to me.

I turned and our eyes met. At that moment I wanted to kiss her, but was too shy to make a move. She sensed my desire and moved closer. Our lips met, our hands explored, and we made love. For both of us it was the first time with a woman. Our joy was so welcome, yet so strange. It wasn't so much a conscious choice as it was a realization. It felt so right to love a woman, yet we felt guilt and shame for having tasted the forbidden fruit.

Even though we decided not to tell anyone, our actions spoke clearly. We spent every free moment together. Our happiness spilled out without conscious knowledge. Even though friends started acting strangely and conversation would cease when we entered a room, I knew I could not stop caring for her. I had taken the step and would never go back.

Carol Lemieux
Medford, Massachusetts

Invoking the Harvest Moon

When I was a child, a few of my early friendships with other girls progressed into sexual experimentation and seemed a natural evolution of friendship and closeness. I can still vividly recall being surrounded by tall grasses, lying on top of Marie, kissing her passionately, and loving the feel of her body beneath mine.

During this time, I felt very self-confident. I was a tomboy who loved being outdoors, climbing trees and exploring the surrounding fields and the lake area where I grew up in Ohio. I played baseball, volleyball, and badminton and acted out mini-dramas which I made up. I loved animals and had a menagerie of dogs, cats, birds, a rabbit, and even a snake. I voraciously read novels, biographies and autobiographies about famous women's lives and the difficulties and choices we faced (Clara Barton, Harriet Beecher Stowe, the Bronte sisters, *Little Women*). These books fed my expectation that women were strong and capable and led interesting lives. I identified with Jo, also a tomboy, and one of my favorite heroines from *Little Women*. Jo took a strong leadership role in her family, as I did in mine.

I also felt a deep appreciation for the magical, nurturing qualities of nature and often spent the late-summer evenings outside, watching as the wind danced her way through the leaves of the trees surrounding our backyard and garden. With the comforting sounds of Lake Erie's waves rolling onto the nearby shore and crickets chirping incessantly in the distance, I sat for hours, mesmerized by the vast, magnificent panoply of stars. While I had attended various church services and youth groups, nothing in that man-made religious realm ever equaled the spiritual high and healing I experienced communing with nature. The tranquility and beauty of nature were available without cost and played an important role in the early shaping of my life and values. There was a need to separate my mind from my body and my spirit. Through my love of nature, I found inner strength, an ability to trust my own inner wisdom, and belief in myself.

Two incidents which greatly influenced my life occurred at about this time, one when I was thirteen and the other two years later. The first incident happened during a family visit, when a female cousin and I were discovered kissing. Her brother loudly reported our activities to our parents, and though nothing more was ever said, it was several years before I saw this cousin again.

When I was fifteen, in the midst of a traumatic family crisis, my alcoholic stepfather accused my mother of being a lesbian. This was the first time I'd heard the word lesbian used. It was also the first time I realized that loving another woman could be considered sick and perverted. Any sexual attraction or crushes on women I'd known had evolved from admiration and affection, and had never seemed wrong or unhealthy. I was stunned. I did not discuss this with anyone and though I never really accepted such a definition, as the adult child of an alcoholic, I also didn't challenge it. Children of alcoholics learn to deny their reality and instincts in order to keep the family intact. Confused and depressed for several years, I worked hard to shift gears and fit in, but I found this excruciating. The usually gangly, awkward surge of adolescent sexuality was complicated even further by my denial of a significant part of my identity and feelings.

Later, as an adult, I again began to feel a strong desire to act on my attraction to women, but by this time I had married and separated and was now a single parent. It took several years to work through my fears and anxieties about how being a lesbian would change all of our lives. Would I lose my children in a court battle? How would they feel about my "difference"? Could we survive the stress that such a shift might engender? Over time it became clear to me that the need to love and be loved by another woman was simply not something I could sacrifice for anyone, even my children. I had to trust that somehow we would be able to work it through.

At the age of thirty-one, I returned to school to finish my degree and become a psychotherapist. During this period in the mid-seventies, the feminist movement had gained momentum and most of the women I knew, including myself, were going through enormous changes. Through reading and discussing feminist literature and theory with women friends and relating this new information to my own life experiences, I felt a profound shift. I acknowledged a deep dissatisfaction with my relationships with men — the power imbalance, the disability most men have regarding communication and doing the emotional and psychological housework necessary to sustain relationships.

As part of my adult degree program, I participated in a group for feminist therapy training which was held on Chappaquidick. Before leaving for the training, Bob, the man I was involved with at the time, mentioned that he wanted me to meet a good friend of his, Jim, and his wife, Alice. He hoped that we would hit it off. As it turned out, Alice would also be participating in the training group.

Packing for my new adventure, I felt a great sense of excitement and anticipation. I had a strong feeling that this would be a turning point in my life and had recently declared myself open to the possibility of a relationship with a woman.

Arriving at the estate where the training was to be held, I saw a dark-haired, slender, green-eyed woman talking animatedly and I instinctively liked and felt drawn to her. She complained about teaching part-time at a local college and about the difficulties of raising two teenage daughters, but it was clear from her laughter and attitude that she really enjoyed it immensely. She seemed restless and unable to remain in one spot for long, gesturing with a lit cigarrette in hand. As she turned to help greet newcomers, we said hello and she introduced herself as Alice.

As it progressed, the training was both exhausting and exciting. We also had time to play and relax after several days of intense workshops and meetings, some of which participants facilitated. One night the entire group decided to stage a party. We discussed this possibility with a great deal of flirtatious and outrageous banter. This was destined to be a coming out celebration for several of us.

In comtemplating the party that evening, I did something I did a lot then: I tested the water before taking the plunge. I was aware that I wanted to get to know Alice better and that I needed to know if she felt the same, but I couldn't admit why or what it meant.

So what did I do? Did I go to the party and ask her to walk with me near the ocean while the bewitching full moon in the night sky lit our way? Did I deal directly with the issue and tell her of my attraction and desire to get to know her? No. Instead, I skipped the party and remained in my room reading. I needed some focus to channel my energy, because by then I was bouncing off walls. I spent a very long night waiting until I could see her again the next day.

Waking up early the next morning, one of the first things I became aware of was the distinct, high-pitched sound of her voice. I couldn't wait to get downstairs, but I sure took my time, making a casual entrance. After slowly descending the stairs to the dining room and taking in the wonderful smells of breakfast cooking, we exchanged tense greetings. She made an innocuous comment and then asked why I hadn't made it to the party the night before. I told her that I'd been really tired and had decided to read instead.

In the training session that morning, we were asked to team up with somebody with whom we had a conflict. Alice and I quickly found each other (we were standing next to one another) and decided to do something physical rather than verbal. The exercise was to push against each other, palm to palm, in an attempt to move one another from the spot where we had rooted.

The intensity and energy between us was exhilarating! She was furious that I hadn't attended the party, and was not afraid to let me know it. That was all I needed to know. I suggested that something was happening between us and we agreed to spend our free time that afternoon together on the beach.

Later, taking deep breaths of pungent ocean air to calm my racing heart, I found myself stealing glances at this woman lying on the beach next to me. She talked for hours about her husband Jim, her daughters, about the perils of teaching part-time, and the women she'd been attracted to. I told her about my children, my art work, my degree program, and my previous relationships.

Our attraction to each other quickly escalated. That night we slept on the living room floor of the main house, since we were both housed in small bedrooms with other roommates. We talked far into the morning. I wanted to take home with me an indelible memory of everything about her — her musky, sweet body perfume, the sensual curve of her barely muscular arms, and the satin softness of that first touch of her full breasts. Her eyes, often half-shaded in self protection, were like laser beams, emitting a myriad of emotions and colors.

With that first kiss and touch, my senses were acutely heightened. Everything seemed to happen in slow motion. Acknowledging the fantasies and yearnings which had been kept in check for years and crossing that artificial barrier to her body and psyche were tumultuous. The release of feeling and emotions, of the desire to be held close and ultimately to be loved by another woman was a magical, extraordinary moment — coming home to something that I had needed for so long, yet denied.

Our training workshop ended the following day. Having had little sleep, but high on our life-altering, newly developed intimacy, we wasted little time in talking to the group about our attraction. We needed to be enfolded and affirmed by this large body of women, and we were. The meeting ended with my naming the other women from the group I'd found attractive. My favorite of our four facilitators commented in a concerned way that she was surprised by the number of women I'd named.

Traveling back to Boston, Alice and I were invited to spend the night at the home of one of the other participants who lived with a lesbian couple. We jumped at the opportunity to prolong the return to our usual lives, and indulged in a second night together. We slept in a single bed in a small room, surrounded by feminist posters on the walls and seashells on the night table to remind us of our Chappaquidick origins. With August moonlight blazing through the open third-floor window, I learned that night why men are both entranced and intimidated by our bodies. I also learned to have much more appreciation for my own.

Eight participants from the training group formed an ongoing support group. At least two other group members eventually came out, and Alice and I were credited with showing them the alternative to Bob and Carol and Ted (or Jim, in this case) and Alice.

Initially, after returning to our everyday realities and struggling to fit one another into our jam-packed, overly committed lives, our relationship was exhilarating. We stimulated in each other a wonderful, creative exchange of ideas and energy. We also supported one another in managing our families after we both separated from the men who had been part of our lives. As both parents and working students (Alice eventually also returned to school), it was simply overwhelming to add to our already tense lives the stress of dealing with newly forming identities and the problem of maintaining friends and community ties, as well as managing the conflicts in our relationship. There were money and class differences between us which we found difficult to confront. Finally, we were both adult children of alcoholics. I grappled with trust issues and a terror of commitment I neither recognized nor understood then. Eventually, we separated very painfully.

Yet now, with some distance, most of what I remember is that through loving each other as we did, we offered a mirror, one to the other, through which to see ourselves in whole new ways. In loving her, I eventually recognized the absolute necessity for learning better how to understand, love, and empower myself.

▼

Andrea Freud Loewenstein
Boston, Massachusetts

New Mountain

This essay is actually an excerpt from a novel, *Letter from Sara*, that I wrote in 1974, when I was in the throes of my first passionate love affair with a woman — I should say first *fully consummated* love affair, because I was certainly passionate enough before that.

In high school, I used to expend the best part of my energy on courting my young women teachers. Courtship is an art all its own, and I was good at it. I knew how to select gifts that were just right; not expensive enough for my teacher to feel she had to return them, but special. I'd give flowers I'd picked myself, lilacs or apple blossoms or pussy willows, or an old illustrated copy of her favorite childhood book, which I'd picked up for a song. To court someone properly you have to learn a lot about them, and I was a good and sympathetic listener.

The girls I knew who went out with boys used baseball terms to talk about what they had done on a date: kissing was first base, touching of the breasts was second, and so on. I had my bases too. When a girl had asked me to call her by her first name I'd know I'd reached first. When she told me I could drop by her apartment, that was second. A home run meant holding her in my arms while she cried about her cruel boyfriend. That was going all the way as far as I was concerned, and I managed it two or three times.

So you see, there was plenty of passion. I knew from the very beginning that passion was what you had for women, but I thought sex was what you did with men. Joanna was not the first woman I slept with. There were others for whom I must have been very disappointing, because I couldn't unlearn this separation I'd mastered so well. But when I fell in love with her, I found out that I could have them both at once, sex and passion, and that's why this piece sounds so adolescent, even though I was twenty-four at the time, and had been semi-married to a very nice man for three years.

Re-reading it now, I'm tempted to make changes — to take out all those spirals and circles inside circles inside flames and being reborn. But I wasn't thirty-seven then, I was twenty-four going on fourteen, and fourteen-year-olds in love tend to write in clichés.

I never published that novel, which may be just as well. There was a whole rash of them about that time, hot and naive coming out stories full of circles and shells and love that was mostly projection but sure felt good. I was grateful for them then, and for the new, exciting community they came out of, a community which nurtured me through my second adolescence so warmly and well. Some of them still work now, but I don't really think we need another one. But I haven't thrown *Letter From Sara* away, either. When I go back and read what I wrote then, I feel affectionate and protective; the kind of feeling I might have for a little sister dyke. It feels good to be publishing something I wrote during that time when the world was round in a whole new way and I knew it was never going to be flat again.

In this chapter Joanna and Sara, who have known each other for only a week, take a trip to Sara's grandparents' house in the Berkshires:

We left the next afternoon for New Mountain. Joanna had time to rent herself a pair of cross-country skis, which I already had, and I had time for a brief but unpleasant scene with my mother: "You're leaving, just like that, right after you got home? Not that I care,

I'm too busy anyway. Who is this woman anyway, another one of your crazy lesbian friends? Mark was such a nice person. I always thought so. I know what I thought! Is that the newest, that I'm not allowed to have any thoughts? Please — excuse me for breathing. Don't let *me* stop you, go right ahead and ruin your life, it's too late anyway."

We left the next afternoon in my old Ford covertible with two pairs of cross-country skis and a paper bag full of food. I decided to leave my mother's curse behind once we got into the car together. It was stepping into a fantasy, and I decided I should be allowed to leave behind anything I wanted to. It worked pretty well, except that I kept waiting for the clock to strike midnight and have everything disappear, or to turn back into a frog. Joanna felt the same way. "Where's the kick?" we kept asking, right from the beginning. We were right, of course; it came in the end. We just got away with it a little longer than you usually can.

Driving up to New Mountain is always exciting. The closer I get, the more familiar it feels, and the more lonely and isolated the scene becomes. There is a gradual climb, and at a certain point, right at a small clearing in the woods which has two white gravestones, my ears always pop, and that means that we are almost there. I didn't have to tell Joanna how it felt to be getting closer, because by looking at her face as she drove I could tell that she felt it too.

The driveway was all snowed up, so we had to walk half a mile in through the deep snow; there was the house, small and green and white, quietly waiting. I got the key from its place in the woodshed and we went in. And then I thought that the kick was really happening because the furnace didn't work. We were already freezing and the furnace was essential, and nothing we did would make it go on. I kicked it finally, and looked at Joanna, who was standing there in her tight knitted cap and blue navy jacket and I thought, *I'll never get to make love with her now, never*, and moaned aloud.

Then I went to the phone and called up my grandfather, Opa. Once, in junior high school I sent him a poem I had written, about wishing I could miss school to be out in the woods, and he sent me one that he had written in response. It was about nature and peace, and he had written it in English for me. And now, Opa told me how to make the furnace work. "So, Sarachen, you find the small button inside the door, yah? You are not alone there?"

"No Opa, someone is here with me." Which was obvious, as I was yelling whatever he told me to Joanna, who was in the hall with the furnace. She'd yell back, "Okay, what next?" when she'd done something. My grandfather is a wonderful man, and for all her intensity, Joanna can be a damned competent woman. All of a sudden that furnace started whining. It thumped a few times, and then it was breathing for good. I shouted out some ecstatic thanks to Opa, put down the phone, and hugged Joanna. It was going to be real, after all.

Once we had the necessity of heat, we could concentrate on other things. I went into the kitchen to unpack the food and heat up our dinner, while Joanna went out to get some wood to make a fire in the fireplace. The three hours in the car was the longest time we'd spent together since we'd met, and it was good to be in the kitchen alone, making toast and heating soup, bumbling around in my own way and listening to Joanna moving with her soft elegant strides, like a deer or a wildcat, in the other room.

When I came in she was bent closely over the fire, arranging the sticks carefully. They were just catching, filling the room with the strong, sweet smell of slightly wet wood, and she leaned nearer to it, and seemed to speak to the flames. They listened, and so we sat by the fire and ate, and then drank some sherry from Opa's store. The liquid was the same amber color as Joanna's hair as it reflected the flames. We hardly touched at first, and when we did it was by accident, our backs brushing as we both huddled by the fire. Then we turned and Joanna touched my face lightly, with the tips of her fingers, like a blind person learning by touch; first my cheeks and the hollows under my eyes and the lines on my forehead, then my lips, and then she tilted my head up a little, and we kissed. I felt like a child all through this, helpless and open and wet. A wall inside me had vanished and another force had come to life, a deep circular storm at my center that was different from anything I'd felt before. "Joanna, I feel there's a volcano or a tornado inside me," I whispered to her, childishly.

She laughed softly and said, "I know, I know. I feel it too."

I wanted to make love there on the rug by the fire, or to run into the bedroom with the two double beds pressed together where

Oma and Opa slept in the summer, but Joanna wanted to wait.

"We have time, " she said, and she stared into the fire, gentling my impatience with her stroking hands until the flames had died down and the last coal had become grey.

Then we went into the bedroom, and took off each layer of clothes. I was afraid for a moment because Joanna was so long and smooth and flat, with the firelight still glowing in her skin; I felt big and lumpy and awkward, but it was too cold to stand around naked long. We jumped into bed and pressed together like two children for warmth, and laughed as we rubbed each other's cold feet, and then we stopped. Suddenly Joanna was over me and it occurred to me that she knew me well already, maybe knew secrets of my body that I didn't know yet myself. Her mouth was pressed on my nipples which were newly alive, and then she pressed down hard on me and I came quickly, like a firecracker, before I could stop it, and moaned with disappointment. "Don't worry," she whispered again, close and wet and breathing deeply, "there's time." I made love to her then, wanting to touch her everywhere at once, my mouth moving from her soft tender ear to her nipple, my hand exploring the shape of her cunt, and she came almost as fast as I had, and we lay together laughing and holding each other, and then I felt her breathing get slower and more regular. She was asleep there, in my arms. I held as still as I could and felt the rhythm of Joanna's breathing, the slow, regular pulse of the furnace, and of the whole house. Then I thought I could feel the mountains breathing in and out, and I imagined them around the valley we were in, gentle and snowy and enclosing. There was a sense of everything being connected, big to small, small to big, circles inside circles. I tried to follow the circles around and around and around until I reached the still round dot in the very center that was me, Sara. I knew that when I hit it, I would be asleep. I was.

Our days in New Mountain were not random, but were filled with patterns and ritual which seemed to be there already, for us to uncover and assume. From that evening, Joanna was the fire keeper, and I made dinner. She'd make breakfast, and we'd sit eating it and drinking coffee or hot chocolate for a long time, just talking and filling in our lives for each other. Then we'd go to a place we'd carefully decided on and ski all day. I was the teacher then, since I've been skiing ever since I could walk. I was ceremoniously presented with a tiny pair of skis by Opa, who skied the Alps with my father when *he* was a child. Joanna had never skied before, but she had learned everything I had to teach her by the end of the week. Each of us would be alone for a while when we came back from skiing. We'd sit in separate rooms and write in our journals. I would read after that from an old red-covered copy of *Middlemarch* I'd brought, and Joanna would think, sitting motionless for up to an hour, gazing at some scene only she could see. I saw her that way when I cheated once, looking silently into the room where she sat, and she told me afterwards that she had done the same thing, and had found me so deep inside my book that I didn't hear her even when she tripped at the door. Then we'd wash, and I'd make dinner, and Joanna would make the fire. We'd sit and eat the way we did the first night and then go to bed.

The facts of the week sound so dry, like drops of hail falling into a bucket. It kept snowing off and on, and each of the things I've mentioned was more like a snowflake, really, all intricate and lacy and petalled when you look at it closely. Take the fire: Joanna had the same intricate relationship with each fire she made. I think it was on the third day, after we'd eaten and she had made the fire, that I came in from the kitchen to find her building it up again. I'd just washed, with boiled snow-water in a big pan, and put on a clean shirt and pants. While the fire turned Joanna the color of amber, it made me pink, and I felt rosy and clean and beautiful as I came in. Joanna was in her place by the fire with her knees up and her legs spread apart. There was a place there, inside her legs, where I wanted to be, and when I was there I knew it was right. It was circles inside circles again, the unit the two of us and fire made, the circle of each of us separately and the pulsing one of my cunt, beating in and out like a heart. I reached for my journal and wrote a poem, right there inside Joanna's legs. I read it to her as soon as it was finished.

> I am held inside your circle,
> My head in your lap.
> Your knees, your long legs,
> The length of waist, up to your breast.
> Your arms circle me round.

We watch the fire burning down.
Each red coal contains one flame.
"The coal holds the fire," you say.
"The red coal is the fire."
Now your hand moves down to press
The center of my self.
Down from my lips,
Up from my toes,
My currents reach
The circle your hand knows.
I rock inside you,
Born to myself again.
Outside, one plate of silver stars,
Brittle in the round black sky,
Slowly spins — and spins us home.

By the time we reached the bed that night, I needed to lie apart, trying to calm down. If I had begun the week as a child, learning sexuality all over again, I was an adolescent now and I wanted to go slowly. Even so, I made the first move, getting up on one elbow, leaning over her, making our first long connection with our eyes alone. Joanna smiled luxuriously, and settled back. I kissed her forehead first, that smooth place between her eyes and hairline, and wanted to stay there forever. There was another place I found on her bony shoulders. I licked it and kissed and nibbled and wanted to stay there all night. She reached up and pulled my face down to hers, and kissing was like that too, the country of tongue and teeth a separate thing in itself, the taste of the inside of Joanna's mouth as intimate as the taste of her cunt. I was over her again, our breasts barely brushing together, and then I took her nipples, hard and puckered, in my mouth, her small firm breasts soft on my cheek. She made little noises and reached out and caught all of me and pulled me down on her. "Wait, wait," I told her, but we were pressed together, on our sides now, cunt to wet cunt, our hard pubic bones touching and pressing, our eyes locked together, until I had to pull apart, quickly. "I don't want to come yet," I told her. "I love you, let me make love to you, Joanna." At first I was awkward, wanting so much to know her as she knew me, to be her perfect love, to make her happy, and I felt my hand like a big groping paw, and I wanted to call out her name but it stuck in my throat. She called me back, guiding me down, and my lips grazed past her smooth amber belly and stopped in her wet cunt, my finger knowing to go deep inside her, my tongue finding her clitoris. I felt her movement after a while and then I became it, and didn't have to be told any more, and we moved together, and I wanted it not to end, and she came like a storm, crying out almost painfully. The sound of her made me cry out too, and then her fingers found me and I couldn't wait any more, but looked into her eyes, and came.

Later, I grew up more. As Joanna learned months of skiing in a week, I learned years of sexuality. I kept stretching and stretching, and I learned all over again to wait and time myself, to let the currents build until, with her tongue moving insistently and her fingers thrusting, I exploded in waves, a new Sara with a waterfall inside her — with a whole ocean.

It was as if I'd shed some old skin like a snake, and hardly recognized the self I'd uncovered. Sometimes it was frightening, because I still carried the same set of rules and defenses that I'd stored up for so long in my head, and I wasn't sure where they fit any more. I wanted to make love all the time, for one thing, and Joanna didn't. I knew there was a rule that two lovers were supposed to want each other at about the same time and about the same amount, and that if that wasn't the case you were supposed to hide it, but I had forgotten how to hide things. I'd lie in bed in the morning, before Joanna had woken up, watching the sun coming in through the snow-spattered pine tree in the window, making dappled patterns on Joanna's body, and resolve not to reveal anything when she woke up — just to give her an affectionate, sisterly kiss and jump out of bed. She would wake, then, and I'd forget. And forget again, when she didn't want to make love, that it didn't mean I was hateful and ugly and unlovable.

Once I did jump out of bed, leaving her to drift back into sleep. I took the red blanket and my journal, and went and sat in the room called the breakfast room, which was made mostly of windows, and watched the rabbits hopping across the untouched new snow, leaving their little tracks, which were covered up right away again by the wind drifts. The mountains seemed binding instead of cradling, and I wished I could be the rabbits, could leave the way they did. I wrote a poem then, which I called "Hare in Winter," because the word rabbit didn't seem elegant enough for a poem.

I have moved startled
From the power of your eyes
Stepped sideways, skittish
With disbelief,
An animal, who having learned
Early and long of human treachery
Keeps always half herself
Awake, aware, ready
To spring away
I have paused, tenuous
In mid-flight,
Scanning, sniffing behind
The sound of your soft words,
Snatching the bait I want
Before the snare can snap.
I am a hare in winter,
And, though I warm myself with you,
I keep on sensing danger.
My long ears quiver
With minute sounds.
I come in to you
But keep an open window
Close at hand.
Outside, a snowy field
Stretches, wide and free.
The quick, quick weight
Of my running feet
Will hardly break
Its crust.

The writings were a part of the unbinding too, a part of the waterfall, those journal entries and poems that kept coming out of me all that week, and they helped me to keep up with a growing that was almost too fast.

It was painful for Joanna too, although I think her pain was not as much connected with me as with the private, nightmare places she visited alone from time to time. Once, as we sat quietly by the fire, she grew ice-cold and remote and I knew, although she was wordless, that she'd gone somewhere else, to a place she hated and was afraid of. I couldn't follow her there, but I held her, and tried to let my warmth go into her, and talked to her in small comforting words, and after a while I felt her coming back again. "Nobody's ever done that", she whispered to me. "Stayed with me and brought me back. Everyone was always too scared of getting caught themselves . . ."

"But it's your nightmare, not mine," I told her. "There's no way it could catch me, only my own can do that."

Joanna's nightmare places seemed to be full of padlocked iron doors; jail cells or hospital rooms guarded by deadly, white-coated men were strange to me. There were no men in *my* dark places, only women, and sometimes Joanna herself, holding out arms of infinite warmth and loving, and then vanishing, or changing, laughing at me hatefully before her disappearance.

Although these things were there, hovering around our edges during the week, our combined powers were always strong enough to chase them away after a short time. I dreamed that Joanna revealed to me a monstrous trick, that she had been using me for some kind of evil magic. I woke up trembling and suspicious. She had been up for hours, watching the sun rise, and thinking of me. She had just come back to bed, freezing and happy and so passionate that my dream shattered and dissolved as I told the first awful part of it into the softness of her neck. We lay together for a long time that morning, and I felt something inside me heal. Afterwards, sitting in the breakfast room again, I felt sticky, as if I had been swimming in the ocean, and I licked my arms and found that I loved the taste and smell of me. Then Joanna brought in perfect soft-boiled eggs, and English muffins and butter and coffee and hot chocolate, and we sat across from each other and ate and talked. I remember sitting there, dipping my muffin into the chocolate, listening to Joanna earnestly discussing the relative merits of the open field and the woods for our days skiing, and telling myself, "This is how it feels to be joyful. I must never, never forget."

On the last day we skied both woods and fields. Breaking

through trees to the open, we saw a family of deer — a doe and three fawns — running lightly across. We followed them, going lightly too, over the snow's surface, and Joanna said that for the first time, she really felt a part of her skis. "It's a whole different way of moving!" she said. "Like those deer!" When we found a long gentle slope on the field, she skied down it again and again, as if she wanted to stop time, to fix it right there. I stood at the top, watching her, and writing another poem in my head.

> She leans
> Into the hill,
> Its long curves mirroring
> Her contours.
> Her mother hill
> Accepts her easy,
> Gives her a long, smooth curving
> Way down.
> Her ski tracks stretch behind her,
> Connecting—
> Start to finish,
> And her to me,
> Still waiting on the hilltop,
> Willing that my love
> May hold her, gentle, easy as the hill
> And willing that the risk she takes with me
> Will be as constant, joined with good connections
> As this, her long
> Cross-country
> Downhill run.

I cried all the way back to Boston. It was painful, but the tears felt good, and I liked the sound of my crying and salty taste in my mouth. I cried when it was my turn to drive, and again when I sat next to Joanna as she drove, with my head on her shoulder. She sat still and frozen, wordless again. She wrote me later that she didn't cry until three days after I left, after she first realized I was really gone, and I had been lucky or wise to have done it there, while we were still together.

Sandra Luders
Greeley, Colorado

Ahead of the Game

I was born in a small town in south-central Kansas of very conservative parents with a Baptist, Methodist, and Quaker background. It was a loving home, yet strict almost to the point of being rigid. I learned more don'ts than do's, and definite male/female roles with a double standard in many areas. Being a sensitive, obedient child, I complied, yet always had a gnawing feeling within that something was different about me.

Although I'd been taught "queers" and "homos" were doomed to Hell, I often came to the defense of someone who was accused of being different. I was guilty of remaining quiet or going along with a joke about "them" as I got older, lest anyone dare accuse *me* of being "one of them."

I adored my grandfather, my mother, and brothers, and dated a lot through high school. I love my sons and son-in-law, and have over the years had some wonderful male friends, yet was drawn to several of my women teachers. I felt an unspoken bond with them yet could never really express it. I was afraid of being scorned for having a close relationship with someone of the same gender and I wasn't really able to label what it was that I was feeling. It was not until 1982, at the age of forty-six, that I even heard the word lesbian. And it was a shock to me to realize that I was one!

Although I had complied with my parents' wishes and got married, it wasn't right and I knew it. I told my father that I didn't love Don and couldn't go through with the marriage, but Dad said, "That's all right, you'll *learn* to love him!" Then he firmly took hold of my hand and we marched down the aisle. I felt like I, or at least a large part of me, died that day.

It was a stormy marriage, really more like a cold war. My minister said Don seemed to have something against women, and my sister said, "Sandy, it's obvious you don't love Don, but really bad when you don't even like him!" With all the prompting and advice from well-meaning friends and relatives we continued in the relationship, and I really tried hard to be a loving, devoted wife, but something was missing. We had six beautiful, healthy children: a son, who is now twenty-seven-years-old and in the military; a twenty-five-year-old daughter, who is married and had her first child in July 1987; a twenty-four-year-old daughter who is in the process of a divorce; a twenty-year-old son and daughter; and a seventeen-year-old daughter. I thoroughly enjoyed my children, yet at times was frustrated and angry inside.

My first experience with an openly gay person was at work in a correctional facility. I was very drawn to a woman prisoner, Kelly, and she to me, although she was only six months older than my oldest child. When Kelly was released, I managed to get her released into my custody, because I had grown to love her and wanted to see her as much as possible. Making love with her was my initiation into the gay world and it was wonderful! I couldn't imagine feeling so loved and so close to anyone. It wasn't just the act of sex, with all of its overtones, it was actually loving, caring and sharing!

The relationship began to sour within six months as Kelly was extremely possessive. She resumed drinking and using other drugs, staying out with both men and women and lying to me about it all. I told her to leave, that our relationship was over, and she threatened to tell my children, friends, parents and co-workers. I had a high-paying, high-profile job, a home, family, friends and didn't want to risk it by letting them know, so she stayed, but the relationship died. Still, I knew she had stirred something in me that could no longer be denied. I was, and am, a lesbian!

I met a young woman at a party Kelly and I had gone to and we spent the whole evening talking. She was struggling to get over a relationship and mine was over, yet we felt the time wasn't right for either of us to express any more than friendship. We simply enjoyed each other's company that evening and went our way. We never indicated to each other that there was any attraction. Ten months later, I ran into Cyndy again. Although Kelly was still around, I was no longer allowing her to dictate who I would or would not see, so Cyndy and I began to go out for coffee and eventually I had the courage to physically remove Kelly from my home.

I loved Cyndy and wanted to tell my parents about us. It seemed the natural thing to do, to tell people you love about that significant person in your life. I was recuperating from lung surgery and Cyndy moved in with me and helped nurse me back to health. When she brought me home from the hospital, the phone rang as we walked in the door, and I answered it. It was my mother and she said, "Oh, it's you! Is that woman there with you?" I affirmed that Cyndy was there and Mother said, "You are no longer a part of this family! As long as you continue to live like that we never want to see you or hear from you again. You are not welcome here. Don't call, write, or even come back to this town, or try to get in touch with anyone else in the family."

I sort of expected it, yet it was devastating! To have family and friends drop me as though I didn't exist. Cyndy was shocked; she had never met such opposition before. She said, "Tell them to fuck off!" I told her I couldn't do that because that wasn't my style. I refuse to sink to the level others may descend to. I have and will continue to write letters and send cards to family on special occasions, and be who I've always been.

Acknowledging my sexuality hasn't changed my moral code, my belief in God, my work ethic, my caring for other people, or my interest in living life to its fullest. I believe the biggest obstacles to accepting myself as a lesbian have been the rejection of my family and friends, and my religious background.

Cyndy has helped me in that struggle to recognize the woman in me, and see that my sexuality is only another part of me. Cyndy's family has had a much better reaction to our relationship. Her mother and brother accept and love us both very much and we love them. This has been a big boost to us as well as the many gay friends Cyndy had, and new friends we've found together. We've also been supported by some new, non-gay friends. Cyndy got a job in Pennsylvania just three months after we bought a home together in 1986. The 1,800-mile separation hasn't been easy, but we are a committed couple and have been together three and a half years. We hope to be together another ten, twenty, or thirty years.

We've had some difficult times both financially and emotionally, but have sought counseling separately and together, which has proved invaluable. Since Cyndy is a counselor, she has taught me to share what is going on inside, keeping the lines of communication open. Reading self-help books and sharing those with each other, sharing household duties, allowing quiet time for each other have also been helpful.

If we're feeling pressured by each other, I've learned to say, "Back off!" Cyndy has always been very verbal and has encouraged me to become more assertive, while I've helped her to see that two-by-four therapy is not always the way to handle a situation or another person.

We take an interest in each other's work and goals, are proud of one another's accomplishments and growth, encouraging each other as much as we can.

We have our own ideas about a lot of things, but we try to blend our differences or allow them to expand our relationship. I love children, she can't stand them, but is trying to become more tolerant of them. I can see a softening in her about many things. She has a gentleness about her, although she is no pushover. We're becoming accustomed to one another's moods, likes and dislikes: we have become separate, yet one. Neither takes the other for granted, and we respect each other's need for privacy and time alone, then coming together again, refreshed. We believe you can have a good, workable relationship if you truly love and are willing to give and forgive.

In the last few years, my family has even begun to come

around. At my father's funeral in 1986, I was finally able to talk at length with my brother and he said, "Sis, if you've found someone you love, who loves you, go for it, because you are way ahead of the game."

I also found that three of my sister's five children accept Cyndy's and my relationship and that I'm still their Aunt Sandy. My mother and I have re-established a pretty good relationship, primarily because I understand where she's coming from and try not to push anything on her.

My younger son has accepted our relationship, although he doesn't understand it. He just sees that I'm happy. He finally told his girlfriend about us after he'd been dating her for over a year. She smiled sweetly and said, "Yes, I know." He said, "Nicole, how long have you known?" Nicole replied, "Since before we started dating, and I think your mother is neat. I can't believe you'd be mean that long, Aaron! It's about time you told her you love her." What a relief for both of us!

Stephanie, my twenty-four-year-old, has sought some counseling and has come to accept me. Although she doesn't understand Cyndy's and my relationship, she tells Cyndy she loves her too, and it shows.

My other daughters, Lisa (25) and Michelle (20), are coming around as well. They are speaking to Cyndy and acknowledging us as human, although they don't understand. My oldest son, Eric, (27) says he is still dealing with it and that he may choose to never accept or understand, but he does love me and always will.

I've come to believe that love, time, and your own caring and understanding of others' feelings can and will make a difference. By being the best you can possibly be, your sexuality will fade in the minds of others as not being the most important part of you, but a part of the whole. God bless you in your quest for your "self."

Judith McDaniel
Albany, New York

Ten Years of Change

Fragments: At the Beginning
(1965, Exeter University, England . . . Journal Notes)

3 May . . . Carolyn and I were discussing my novel — she really takes it quite to heart — I suggested at one point that the 'slow, steady woman' should in reality be a lesbian, and I thought she was going to call out her lawyers. It helps me, though, to take my writing seriously because she does . . . Tonight I remembered for a moment from last fall at Stratford: two Japanese girls — quite sophisticated-looking, but young — holding tightly to each other's hand, one leading, one following — as they worked their way up the theater steps. A longing pang — not allowed in Western culture.

5 May . . . I want her respect — hers and others' — which is the only reason I'm trying to organize my life. It's not easy, but it's worth it. I don't love many people.

12 May ... We were talking about letters this afternoon and how to sign them, etc. Anyway she said there were only three possible ways to close ... "Yours faithfully," "Yours sincerely," and "Love from." I asked which category was I in and she said, "Oh, you're different." Don't know what that meant, but in the future she said I'll get a "Love from."

17 May ... I had some funny ups and downs today. I guess it was from sitting at my desk and working ... then Carolyn was going out and I wasn't, which still galls occasionally. I went in to see Carolyn for a few minutes this afternoon. She had three exams this week, and I knew she'd be busy, but she said so, too — something to the effect of "Well, you'll be on your own for the next three days, you know." Well, I did, but don't like to be reminded of it — nor of the fact that in four more weeks I'll be on my own for good. So I indulged in being depressed and went and had my bath and came back when who should come rapping on the door. I hadn't gone in to say goodnight to her because the light was off, so I knew she must have gotten out of bed to say goodnight ... and that made all the difference. I could have sung.

22 May ... Carolyn and I sat and talked all afternoon. She started out calling me names. I didn't really mind because it's gotten to the point now that for my own preservation I can't afford to believe she's serious. Anyway, at some point I told her how hard it had been for me to watch her and Geoff together — which brought her up short. It's funny knowing someone so well you can say that and know the precise effect it will have. Then we talked about us and how chancy any sort of attempt to establish communication was ... but we seemed to have been successful and, god, it's going to be hard to leave.

23 May ... We talked all day again today. I've never felt so close to anyone. At times I think — panic — exams — and then I think, but does it really matter? Obviously not that much ... We went flower picking tonight under the cover of dark — one of the lesser social sins — it was cold and raining. Brought back lily-of-the-valley, lilac, straw flowers and some other sprays ... there seemed

to be a marked predominance of white ... except for the first rose of summer Carolyn found on a vine and put in the small vase for me — it's pink.

Fragments: Denial

1971, on waking in Jon's bed, a dream: In a kind of a girl's dorm. I am standing with my friend in our room. Across the hall from my room is a bathroom with several stalls. For a while I am inside one of them or else I know what is inside one of them, as I am still across the hall in my room. I keep urging my friend to hurry. Just then someone discovers the girl's body — she is dead. They say she was murdered, but it's my dream and I know it was suicide. I won't go look at her, but I know what she looks like. Now I tell my friend I want to leave quick before the police come or we'll have to wait longer. But she says no, it wouldn't be right. So they come with a stretcher to get the body, but there's not much left. She killed herself by chopping off pieces — a bit at a time — and putting them in the toilet.

1972, July, a self-conscious fantasy: Sometimes I think I would like to have an affair with a woman. I don't know why — it's not curiosity — but I think that something is lacking emotionally in all of my relationships.

1972, October, journal notes: Driving home alone from hearing Adrienne Rich read her poems. She is a force, an intensity, and affects me profoundly. There are many dimensions to her poems. I want to read them over and over. Can you dig it baby on the radio. I feel a sense of loss when I hear poetry like that. Because she is writing for me and I understand her in a way I have never understood the 'great' poets — Yeats, Eliot, etc. Why loss? There must be men who read Yeats and to whom he means as much, perhaps more, than this night meant to me. And I'd never really thought about it, but — she exposes herself in her work and I feel I know her well, like I should be driving home with her. But no man in that audience should feel *just* the way I do — something, perhaps, because her clarity is good — but not exactly as I felt. She is totally honest, but you have to have been there to know the truth.

1973, August, journal notes: I told Phyllis how I felt about Sue, making it sound as though I was horrified and terrified — which part of me is. But her reaction was that of the other part of me — that it was normal and understandable under the circumstances — that it is there under any circumstances more than we allow. And that even if it had gone further it wouldn't be a problem unless I made it that way. I really think that, but somewhere else, I'm fighting awfully hard.

The Process: Saying 'The Word'
(1975, January, one week during teaching a course in "The Women's Voice in Modern Literature")

Monday: *Lesbian* — for two years, more perhaps, I have been unable to write honestly, to write at all. My mind stops there, afraid. I have spoken truthfully to no one. But I may have stopped lying to myself — perhaps. To admit that I do love Sue, that I am physically attracted to many women, would make love to them, do dream of them, have always been more emotionally involved with women — without the ambivalence and fear I feel with a man. I wonder how I seem to the world. I am happier now than I have been for a long time, personally and professionally — many things are good. But things inside me are turbulent, agitated, sometimes I feel like I will crack open from pressure. Having no one to confide in is a problem, but only a small part of it. I have a need to know some things, and no way to inquire. I am relieved to finally be knowing some of this consciously, but it threatens me constantly. (And then I wonder whether it's all in a game I'm playing with myself — a thing I have made up and could just as easily make go away again if I chose. Would I want it to go away? I don't know. Is it real? Or does that matter?) . . . Introduced "Women's Voice" today. Talked about the imposed schizophrenia of the woman intellectual. How I always read books about men and identified with men, "knowing" that maleness was the moral, social and cultural norm, but knowing too that I was female. Or thinking I was. But if Molly Bloom was a woman, I must be a mutant. Some of it was getting too close.

Tuesday: Tomorrow is women and madness — how women keep control, how they lose it, what images they use to imagine it — and other enormities. Phyllis says there are also novels of men who are mad, but I don't agree. Portnoy is not mad, just obnoxious. I am furious. Sue is unhappy. Phyllis says it will be better for me when I get away from here. I am mostly content but very lonely: tired and lonely.

Wednesday: Val called today. She wanted to do an independent creative writing project with me. I don't think the department will let me. I'm talking about creating order tomorrow. I don't need that nearly as badly as I need approval and love. Maybe they follow if or when a women creates her own little ordered enclave? My mind is chaotic, but I'm comfortable with that.

Thursday: I lectured today for one and a half hours. Just once I wish somebody would say, "Wow," or make a connection with this stuff for me. Inappropriate, I guess, since I was talking about the lack of cause and effect relationships in women's lives today.

Friday: I'm going through ... Edwin Hawkins Singers. Sue is here. She was at the Van Duyn lecture. I didn't think she'd come up. She sounded sick on the phone. When I first saw her, looking at her, she seemed strange, not familiar, and not attractive — but at dinner all of a sudden there she was again. There. I wonder what she and Lisa say about me. They both know how I feel about Sue. And whenever we embrace I can feel Lisa watching — not jealous even, but very there — observing.

The Process: What it Means

1975, February: Having Blanche Boyd here was important, but more for me than the class. I hadn't planned on letting a radical lesbian have the last word on "The Women's Voice." The class responded much better to Linda Pastan, who spoke about trying to put her family and poetry together. People had fewer questions for Blanche. The question I had was personal and I didn't even recognize it until last night. We sat in the kitchen drinking brandy until 4 A.M. talking about God knows what — I can't remember, but it was fantastic. But I never asked my question . . . What I want to know from Blanche is, so how did you know? When did you decide you were in fact a lesbian, not bisexual, reacting to a bad marriage, etc. I'm not sure there is an answer, but whenever I have one of my imaginary dialogues with Phyllis, she doesn't believe me and all I have is internal evidence. She probably would believe me, of course. I have this image of announcing to the world (i.e. myself, then Phyllis) that I am a lesbian and having the world pat me on the head, take my pulse, and tell me I'll get over it soon. Obviously I'm not sure yet that I won't. It creates internal tension and I'm afraid if I did talk about it — what? I don't know — afraid it would be real, or it wouldn't? And I'd have to try again with a man.

. . . So many of my students know I'm vulnerable. Some of them will protect me, others see it as a challenge. Ellen came out to the house tonight. She said Pat was telling other students I had propositioned her. Part of me laughed and part didn't. I told her what had happened, how Pat did this seduction number on me for three weeks and finally I said, "Okay, I want you," and she freaked. I'd never seen her nervous or disconcerted until that moment. It was almost worth the risk. Anyway, Ellen is furious with her.

1975, March: For several days now I've been picking up Jill Johnston's book, *Lesbian Nation,* and reading it when I should have been grading papers. I don't know what I would have thought of it last year, but I think now it is an important political statement. At the same time I doubt my own judgment. Jane said the other day that she doesn't fall in love with people much older or younger than herself — something about experience, etc. I thought that was true for a while, but then I think of Sue. I know I'm afraid of Ellen's promiscuity, not her age — at the same time I wouldn't mind some casual sex. I ache just to hold another body. I got drunk at Hillary's last night. I was sitting next to her. It's dumb to let myself get so imaginatively caught up where there's no chance of involvement — when others may notice and she could get really pissed off — and I don't have that many other friends.

1975, April: I want a child, but not a man. I want Hillary, but she is with Tom. I'm not sure I ever felt anything about a man. I wish I knew whether I were terrified of sexuality or heterosexuality. I commit myself to men who seem to be able to control me, and then withdraw emotionally. What an incredible thing it is to realize after all these years that I hated dating, that I was never at ease in social situations when I was expected to dance or date or pick up men or whatever. The thing with Dan was typical. I'd really look forward to the ballet or whatever we were going to do, but I never enjoyed spending time with him, even though we had so many interests in common. On paper, he's perfect, I kept telling myself. But I didn't even like him, and I saw him nearly once a week for over a year. I finally went to bed with him just to see if he'd be more interesting. He wasn't — just embarrassing. I can't think of anybody I was ever comfortable "dating." And the men I've lived with became a kind of torture after a while, each in his own way.

The Process: How it Happened

1975, June: I feel more comfortable with my own body and sexuality now than ever before in my life, whether it's negative — knowing that I never have to sleep with a man again — or the positive — finding a natural and spontaneous expression of my deepest, most intimate feelings. And I can see sources for this in what I was ten years ago, but this doesn't invalidate that ... I don't even have to reinterpret those events; if Carolyn had kissed me that night in the garden in England I couldn't have responded positively, even knowing those feelings were there.

When I first started imagining what it might be like to make love with another woman, the idea terrified and excited me. My story line was pretty vague, a lot of embracing and some movement, a little high-fidelity inhalation, but no technicolor and the lens was comfortably out of focus. Usually I was not even a participant.

Fantasies progressed on three different levels as I became more accustomed to the setting. My waking fantasies were the most fun and moved most quickly. Usually in this scenario a strikingly attractive woman would find me irresistable and allow me to be a passive observer at my own seduction. It seemed an ideal solution at the time — I could learn a few new things without taking the risk of looking foolish or performing badly. I had no access to my sleeping dreams at that time. They were gone before I awoke like the orgasm I hovered on the edge of, but lost with consciousness. The imaginative level I had the most trouble with was the one that came in contact with my everyday life. In all the mundane details of classes and meetings and casual associations, I looked at women with new eyes, but what I was imagining became unimaginable when it was connected with Susan's hands or Carol's hair or Peggy's breasts. I developed a pronounced stammer in certain highly charged emotional situations — like the time in the A&P when I was standing across a grocery cart from Hillary Martin and saw for the first time how incredibly blue her eyes were and felt them looking at the back of my brain.

Meanwhile my less conscious fantasies established a pace and direction of their own. From full-blown scenes of faintly developed seduction, I found myself rerunning fragments and details. The projector would run, stick, rewind, run, stick, rewind, ad nauseum, or at least ad emotional fatigue. In one of these scenes I was standing across from a tall woman with long blonde hair held back by a barrette. Our eyes would meet in a direct challenge and erotic exchange. I would reach across to her hair, run my hand down the nape of her neck and unfasten the clasp of the barrette. As her hair fell forward I would lean to kiss her mouth and the projector would cut off. And cut off again and again.

Finally my real life began to follow my fantasy life. As I became more comfortable with the idea of loving a woman, I gave myself permission to act on those feelings. I stopped waiting for an aggressive woman to seduce me. I stopped asking women I knew would say no. I stopped worrying about how well I would perform. Last night I took Karen's hand and led her back to my bed. About halfway through the final scenario I remembered to ask, "Is this all right?"

"Yes," she said with some surprise, "Oh, yes."

Toni McNaron
Minneapolis, Minnesota

My Personal Closet

That first job was the hardest I will ever have. I was the English Department. That meant I taught three high school classes, in addition to freshman and sophomore courses in the junior college wing of All Saints. Being a perfectionist, I believed each student should write a theme a week. So every weekend for the two years I worked there, I graded and commented generously on some seventy or eighty papers. Students found their voices in my classes and went on to college at some of the "best" schools in the country — all out of the South at my urging.

My students loved me right away and stayed in my classroom after school to talk about eternal verities and other similarly unmanageable topics. But they worked hard at reading, memorizing, and writing about literature by all the major white male authors. As I recall, I did not teach a single female author. Out of class, we spent idle hours walking in the lovely woods surrounding the school or shopping in the tiny town of Vicksburg on Saturday, when they were allowed off campus without a chaperone. My car was a subject of one of their many projects. It was a baby blue

Volkswagen, the first car I'd bought on my own. I'd only made one payment before my arrival. The girls decided it had to have a name and for days worked on possible options. Finally they settled on "Beatrice Portinari," which combined their facination with my story about Dante and his ethereal love-muse-idol, and their loose Latin coining of a word to mean "that which carries McNaron," "Portinari." I was moved by their cleverness and their caring.

One of the high school seniors, Mimi, began spending late afternoons talking about music and nature and how much she adored whichever writer we were studying. Mimi was tall and willowy with shiny, silky-looking dark brown hair that hung down around her shoulders. Her deep-set and bottomless brown eyes looked long and questioningly at me until I was not sure what to do next. She liked French almost as much as English, and gradually I began reading French with her, telling myself I needed to keep up my skill since I was on my way back for more graduate school.

When her teacher assigned Saint-Exupery's *Le Petit Prince* as an extra reading, Mimi jumped at the chance, suggesting that we read it together before compulsory evening chapel. After a day or two of reading at adjacent desks in my classroom, I proposed that we retire to my room on the third floor where we could be more comfortable. Once there, I realized that the only way to be comfortable was to sit on my single bed, since there was only one chair at the small desk provided for letter writing. So tall, willowy Mimi and I began translating a story about a strange and wonderful attachment between a little boy who has fallen from the sky and a fox; a story about taming and being tamed.

Since my dormitory room faced west, our late afternoon sessions were framed by breathtaking sunsets, which we interrupted our translating to watch. Kneeling on my narrow bed, we'd stare out my little oval window, commenting on colors and rays and the beauty of it all. We tried literally to overlook the cannon on the hill. After one such hiatus, Mimi lay down on my bed instead of sitting back on its edge to continue Saint-Exupery. Seeing the last rays of sunlight had made her drowsy, she said. She napped for the fifteen minutes before chapel, while I sat uneasily in the lone chair watching her. I was aware of feelings I'd never had before, which were periodically erased by waves of fear. What did it mean that I looked so tenderly at this student who clearly trusted me or she wouldn't be napping on my narrow bed in the growing dusk? None of my gay male friends' stories entered my mind as I searched frantically for some familiar mooring on which to pin my strange emotions. It never occurred to me that Mimi might be having similar feelings or even be acting in ways that elicited mine. Since I never asked her about her past, I have no idea where I fit in her sexual history.

At the end of the fifteen minutes, she still slept. I realized I had to awaken her or run the risk of missing chapel and being turned in. Attendance was taken of both students and faculty by the Dean of Women, Gladyce Cooper. She stationed herself at the back of the church with a clipboard and several alphabetical lists. If a girl missed a second time, she was denied her shopping or dating privileges for three weeks. If she missed three times, her parents were called for consultation preparatory to asking her to leave. If faculty were absent, Gladyce cornered us somewhere inappropriate like inside a cubicle in the ladies' room. Standing over Mimi as she slept, I broke into a cold sweat. I called to her softly but she seemed not to hear. When I knew that I was going to have to touch her, I gingerly shook her left shoulder with two fingers and saw her eyes open slowly and a shy smile spread over her face. My impulse was either to enfold her in my arms or to run out of the room. Doing neither, I hurried us off to chapel where we arrived as Father Allin was saying the Sanctus. Gladyce erased check marks on two pages, and I registered inside that she not only knew we were late but that we were late together. I felt instantly cautious, angry, and protective.

Within a week of her initial nap, Mimi and I had lain down side by side on my single bed. Sleepy from translation, Mimi had once again reclined for the half-hour before chapel. Tired myself from a long night of paper grading, I joined her, not consciously suspecting what could so easily happen. Again Mimi seemed to drift into a sound sleep, while I lay awake, my mind filled with thoughts and my body with new desires, not present when I had slept with two or three men or even when I had felt passion and tenderness for Malcolm. Over the next month, our progress on the bed went from long soulfull looks to seemingly innocent hugs to a day when our mouths touched and stayed longer than had been my previous experience. No one had ever seemed to want to kiss me deeply nor had I wanted them to. I remember my mild discomfort at 1940s movies when Clark Gable and whoever was his current partner filled the silver screen with their French kisses. Their lips seemed too parted, too moist, too hungry, especially his. But when Mimi and I kissed that first time, all I felt was excitement.

Not surprisingly, Mimi and I became lovers shortly after that first kiss. Neither of us felt awkward or shy about how to make love and neither of us felt guilty about our pleasure. What I cannot remember is what we actually did or how that felt. Sentences I try to write about our frequent meetings are either filled with pulp magazine clichés or read like abstract projections of what two women would do when making love. Though I understand why I cannot bring the sensual details to life, I feel sad and angry. The reason stems from the coincidence of my lovemaking with bi-monthly visits to the school director's office. Though I did not let Father Allin's persecution keep me from Mimi, I internalized enough of it to block out the pleasure and satisfaction connected with my first lesbian relationship.

For most of the years between my involvement with Mimi and writing this essay, I felt guilt and shame about our relationship. I saw myself as the initiator of all our activities and felt vaguely dirty for that fact. Finally I am able to understand that Mimi had her part in the process, that she was eighteen and I was twenty-one, though there was a genuine power differential since I was her teacher. But when we became sexual, I distinctly recall that she was not at all surprised or awkward — facts about myself that I've used as signposts of my inherent lesbianism, but which did not function so to define her until recently.

Our initial setting for sexual delights was the logical place: my bed. But not even faculty doors in the dormitory had locks. Mimi and I began to feel anxious and interrupted our delight when we heard or thought we heard footsteps outside or someone turning the door handle. Once we were barely able to spring up and rearrange our clothing before a student came in to ask me about some poem of Alexander Pope's. She had not bothered to knock, and I felt the same way I had as I saw Gladyce Cooper erase her check marks in chapel: watched, suspected, guilty without quite knowing of what. After that narrow escape, I determined to find a more private, preferably lockable, place for us.

But before I located such a haven, I was called into the rector's office. John Maury Allin was his name, and he later became presiding Bishop of the Episcopal Church of America. That morning in 1958, he tried to preside over my dismissal, but I refused to cooperate. He told me that a student had come to him with a "sickening story" of having seen me the previous evening kissing Mimi in the back of the chapel. My immediate response was "Call her in and have her say that to my face." Maybe I'd read of such scenes in novels and remembered the stoolie's collapsing in the face of the accused. Whatever my model, I was reversing the scene. I was asking the young woman in one of my classes, where I insisted that students name whatever reality they saw in literature, to look me in the face and deny that she'd seen what she had indeed seen. Mimi and I had taken to stealing a goodnight kiss in the foyer of the chapel. We'd stay at prayers until everyone was gone and then meet quickly for a few words and some small gesture of endearment.

Father Allin agreed to the meeting, but stipulated that Mimi must be present as well, clearly hoping that she'd give us away. While he sent for the informant, I rushed to the student lounge which was in a separate building called the Play House. Finding Mimi smoking with her choir friends, I pulled her aside and told her of our plight, that she would have to submit herself to the interview with Father Allin and the as-yet-unknown student. When we all had assembled, it was hard to gauge whose fear and anxiety was the greatest. The student looked at me, burst into tears, and stammered something about being mistaken or exaggerating or mistaking us for someone else. Allin was stymied, which angered him, so that his was the face that reddened. But his only choice was to send us all away.

Since I never spoke to the student who had seen me and my first lover kissing, I have no idea why she took back her story, why she chose in that split-second to side with me rather than the man in authority over us both. The shame I felt at the time, tacitly asking her to lie, I carried with me for many years. Today I am willing to imagine that the young woman simply preferred to help me and Mimi rather than placate a father figure. I had only taught her for a few weeks when the scene took place and do not remember her name. But I owe her my job, since if she had stuck to her story, I would most probably have been forced to leave. Mimi might well have been placed in a difficult position or suspended, though the good rector could have kept her in school by saying that I was the corrupting influence.

Over and over that year, as he continued his accusations, the scenario went something like this: I would get a note from Father Allin or he'd stop me in the hall as I was returning to class from lunch or he'd have Gladyce tell me that he wished to see me at such-and-such a time. Steeled against what was to come, I would enter his office and have the door shut firmly behind me. I always waited for him to lock it, since his office did have the capacity for privacy. Usually we were alone, though sometimes Gladys was there with her ubiquitous clipboard. Twice we were joined by the Dean of Academic Affairs, Wade Wright Egbert, who not only liked me, but thought me a superb teacher. Father Allin opened each of these grillings with the same phrase: "Toni, I'm going to have to ask you to leave if you don't change your behavior. You're corrupting the young and I can't allow that." His fantasies of what I was doing must have upset him a great deal, because by the end of this brief opener his face would be covered with ugly blotches, making him even more unattractive than he was. He resembled a bulldog, with a very thick neck, tiny eyes too closely set in his face, and fulsome lips that snarled when he spoke. My responses were pretty uniform too, ranging from "I don't understand what you're talking about," when he was general in his condemnation, to "But you have no evidence so you can't fire me," when he mentioned Mimi specifically. Once when he was particularly vicious, Wade intervened, reminding him of my excellent work with my students, bringing hard evidence in the form of their devotion to literature, their memorization of endless lines by numerous poets, their long cogent papers written and copiously responded to every week. He also reminded his boss that I was the only English teacher they had and it would be impossible to replace me in mid-year. Father Allin sputtered and fumed, but backed off for that interview. My gratitude to Wade was expressed in renewed efforts to do my job superbly; my students thrived while I consistently gained weight, drank too much, and slept poorly.

My initial confrontation with Father Allin heightened my sense of urgency about finding a private place for Mimi and me to meet. A place presented itself within the next week. My classroom was across from the library in the basement of the main building. It led, through a narrow corridor, to piano and chorus practice rooms — a fact which gave me pleasure many a night as I sat grading papers. In that corridor were two doors: one to a toilet and the other to some unknown space. Upon looking inside the second door, I found a tiny room full of trash, part of an oil furnace, and a small metal box in which lay a lead key. Our school had a security system comprised of several of these little boxes strategically located on campus. Each evening, an elderly watchman patrolled the grounds, checking in at each watch box by inserting its key into a round clock slung over his shoulder. I never figured out how that activity could possibly alert him to anything amiss, but the watchman was quite faithful.

I decided to make that little room our place, though it had neither lights nor a window. Every night for two weeks, I went directly to my classroom after supper, ostensibly to grade papers. Part of each session was spent filling my two wastebaskets plus the ones in each empty practice room with as much trash as I dared without raising the janitor's suspicions. Finally, the room was empty of debris. I cleaned it as best I could, installed a padlock on the inside, gave Mimi the second key, and hoped for the best. What I'd not taken into account was the watchman's schedule of rounds and his need to be able to reach into our room, take out the watch key, and perform his little ritual with the winding clock. We had to delay using our lair until I'd spent another week, ostensibly grading papers, but actually registering the exact time he arrived at that station.

When I felt all was under control, I invited Mimi in for our first evening in privacy. I'd bought flowers, though it was too dark to see them. There, in that literal closet, in constant fear of the curious or fatal knock, my gentle and first lover and I talked and cried and made love. By and large, my scheme worked, though we had narrow escapes. The worst was the appearance of the watchman fifteen minutes before his appointed time. We were lying on our clothes making love; I was experiencing as I always did the sheer luxury of that, compared to our contoured squirming amidst skirts, hose, garter belts, underpanties, and blouses. I recall Mimi's having just laughed softly at something I'd said about her body's resembling a flower — we both referred often to the other in terms right out of the English romantic poets. Suddenly the door was tried, then pushed even harder, as if it were assumed that something had mysteriously gotten wedged against it. I motioned for Mimi to grab her clothers and get behind the door. I threw mine on, talking to him all the while about having bought a lock for the room so I could have a little hideaway from all the students wanting to sit in my room and talk after hours. By the end of this outlandish tale, I was more or less dressed and I let him in. He pushed open the door, little aware that right behind it stood a stark-naked student who might at any moment break into a sneeze or cough or laugh or uncontrollable cry of sheer terror. His motions with the lead key were reluctant, as if he sensed my lie. But he finished clocking our station, and must have never spoken to the rector about this strange occurrence, or even about my use of the room.

Once he had left the furnace room, I waited to hear the side door open and close, indicating his exit from that part of the building. Then I motioned Mimi from her porch, and we collapsed into tears and laughter. That near-miss happened in March, and I never really relaxed again, though we continued to meet when our schedules allowed. We never spoke of our escape any more than we spoke about any part of our relationship. But the scene of our touching and kissing and of my discovering something new and powerful about myself in a dark hole intended for garbage haunts me. I still prefer not to make love in the dark, and am reluctant to be sexual in anyone else's house. I have felt extreme anger and extreme sadness that my initial lesbian experience was blighted by circumstances, by my own silence, and by a sanctimonious priest on his way to a bishopric. When gay and lesbian organizations urge us "out of the closet," I wince: that phrase has never held a metaphorical significance for me; it only reminds me of the exact locale for the first nine months of my lesbian life.

▼

Lesléa Newman
Northampton, Massachusetts

The Summer of '83

It was real hot that summer, the summer of 1983. I spent most of my days lying naked on my bed, reading Ann Bannon's *Beebo Brinker* books. That certainly didn't do anything to cool me down. I had just come out two months before, and I wanted a lover more than I had ever wanted anything in my whole life. I'd been straight for twenty-seven years and I knew there was something wrong the whole time. My mistake was that I thought there was something wrong with me. Why didn't I like being with men? Why would I rather go to the movies, go bowling, go to a natural history museum, go anywhere but to bed with them? I had a problem. I always thought that I was with the wrong man, but the *real* problem was that I was with the wrong sex.

So I moved to Northampton, Massachusetts, in December of 1982, where there were more dykes per city block than anywhere else in the world, or New England at least. Within a few months I was *out* — I cut my hair, threw away my brassieres, bought a pair of Birkenstocks, and moved out of my co-ed cooperative house into an apartment with Anita, a dyke of four or five years. In short, I had done everything but *it*, the big *it* that I had only read about in every piece of lesbian literature I could find. I felt like a teenager again, when I was the last virgin on the block. When, oh when, would I ever find a lover?

Anita didn't have a lover either that summer, so we spent a lot of time together *kvetching*, *shvitzing*, and comparing crushes. One day, after reading a particularly juicy scene from *Odd Girl Out*, I announced to Anita that we had to go dancing that weekend at The Girl's Club, a women's bar a few towns away. Neither of us had ever been there before, and somehow that made it safer and scarier than a dance in our own community. I was determined to go to that bar and bring a woman home with me. After all, it was August already, and if the whole summer passed without me kissing a woman, I knew I would just die.

Anita agreed to go Saturday night. To make things even more exciting, she came up with a bet: whoever was first to ask a woman she didn't know to dance would get her laundry done by the loser for a month. Wow. Stakes were high. I sure didn't want to be *shlepping* Anita's smelly t-shirts and shorts to the laundromat for a whole month. But just the thought of asking a woman I didn't know to dance made my knees buckle. "Ask someone you don't think is cute," Anita said. "Then it's not such a big risk, and it won't matter so much if she says no." But what good was that? I didn't want to dance with someone I didn't think was cute. And besides, the possibility of someone saying no hadn't even occurred to me. You mean that once I got up my nerve to ask she could refuse? Now I was even more apprehensive.

Saturday night rolled around, and Anita and I spent about two hours trying on everything we owned, before coming up with perfect outfits: she wore light blue jeans and a black muscle shirt; I wore white pants and a red low-cut top. I had bought all kinds of buttons, which we laughingly pinned on each other: So MANY WOMEN, SO LITTLE NERVE; SOME DO, SOME DON'T, I MIGHT; and START YOUR DAY WITH ME. Of course, as soon as we got to the bar we took the buttons off and hid them in the glove compartment of Anita's car.

The bar was crowded and smoky. To escape the heat, a lot of women were standing around out in the parking lot, including a whole softball team in uniform. I felt really shy walking past all those women who laughed and talked and stood so easily together, some leaning against the parked cars with their hips touching, drinking beers and looking up at the sky. Anita led me inside and we sat down at a little table, listening to the music and watching the women who were dancing. Then we danced together a few times, which was fun, but not exactly what I had come for. *Hell,* I thought, *if I'd wanted to dance with Anita all night, we could have just stayed home and played Michael Jackson records on the stereo.* When a slow song came on, I told Anita I was going to sit at the bar, and she made a motion to follow me. I shook my head. "Anita," I said. "No offense or anything, but if we dance one more dance together, everyone will think we're an old married couple. You go back to our table and I'll go sit at the bar." I looked at my watch. "Let's rendezvous in an hour, okay?" She nodded and left me to meander over to the bar alone.

I sat on a stool with my elbows leaning back on the bar and watched the dancers for a while. A fast song was on now, and I loved watching all those sweaty bodies moving — hips swaying, breasts bouncing up and down, *tuchuses* shaking. *Sigh.* I let my glance wander among the tables lining the dance floor, until it landed on a dark-haired woman sitting alone, smoking a cigarette and nursing a beer.

That was *her.* Something in me just knew it. I studied her closely. She was sitting low in her chair, with her arm flung carelessly across the table, and her legs up on the empty chair across from her. She wore a white button-down shirt and tight black pants. No buttons, no jewelry. She was suave, cool, tough, detached. I didn't know the word "butch" yet, but I knew I liked what I saw.

I continued to watch her for a while, wondering just how I would approach such a woman. Soon her head turned slightly and she looked in my direction. My stomach practically fell to my feet, the way it sometimes does when I ride in an elevator, but I held my gaze. A flicker of a smile crossed her face before she turned away. And before I could move she turned back. This time I smiled.

Why had she looked my way? I'd like to think she could feel my stare burning a hole in her cheek, though later Anita pointed out that the clock was hanging on the wall above the bar right behind me. I guess it doesn't really matter why she looked at me. I was just glad she did, which I guess was obvious, because eventually she came over and asked me to dance. I thought for sure she was getting up to leave, or to go to the bathroom or something, but she very slowly and calmly walked up to the bar, stood right in front of me and said, "Wanna dance?" Just like that.

I nodded and slipped off my stool. She took my hand and led me onto the dance floor. *Oh my God, she'd holding my hand,* I thought as we passed Anita, who was still sitting alone at our table.

We danced two dances together without saying a thing and then what I was dreading and hoping for happened: a slow song came on. She (I still didn't know her name) opened her arms and I gratefully fell into them.

We danced through that song and the next slow one, and let me tell you, she was some dancer. She had both her arms tightly around me and one leg planted firmly between my thighs, rotating in a manner that was driving me wild. And if that wasn't enough, she started planting little kisses down my neck and across my collarbone, which was peeking out of my shirt. I closed my eyes in sheer ecstacy, hoping that Brooke Shields would never stop singing about her "precious love." At one point I looked up and caught sight of Anita still sitting by herself and watching me dance, her eyes practically popping out of her head. I closed my eyes again, letting my body sway and time stand still until the song was over.

After two more fast songs, Mary (I had finally asked her name) asked me if I wanted to get some air. I did, and as we walked out to the parking lot, she took my hand again. I followed her past parked cars with women leaning against them, past some trees, past the lights of the street, towards a darkened corner of a field with a baseball diamond in it. At that point, I would have followed her anywhere. She leaned back against the metal fence and pulled me close to her. *Finally, thank God,* I thought, as her lips met mine. All the reading I'd done, and all the fantasizing, didn't prepare me for the softness and the strength and the rightness of that first kiss. I felt like my whole body was rushing towards my mouth, crying, "More, more!" I got weak in the knees and wet in the pants. My mouth sought hers again and again. "God, you're beautiful," she said, stopping for air, and then pushed her tongue between my teeth once more.

Eventually we found our way back to the bar and Anita and I went home. Mary never became my lover — it seems she was nursing a broken heart and felt it was fine to flirt, but no dessert. And Anita didn't do my laundry for a month either, saying that Mary had asked me to dance, not vice versa, so it didn't count. I maintained that it was my looking at her so hard that brought her over in the first place, so Anita should at least do my laundry for two weeks. But she wouldn't.

That was the highlight of the summer of '83 . . . In the car on the way home from the bar, I'd kept asking myself what in the world ever took me so long? I decided I sure had a lot of kissing and hugging and other things to do to make up for lost time. I'm still working on it.

Liz O'Lexa
Baltimore, Maryland

You Must Not
Be Doing It Right

Coming out is not a singular, one-time event. Whenever we step from being another face in the crowd towards being an individual who has a name and a personality, we're again faced with the decision of coming out. And again and again, as long as we continue to have the defiance to exist. We don't all dye a purple streak down the middle of our hair, quit our job, start a "womyn"-owned business and secede from the patriarchy by embracing lesbian separatism, although I know one dyke who did.

The beginning of my journey was coming out to myself. It happened in 1975, when I was fourteen and my knee touched the knee of the most beautiful woman in my Minneapolis high school, Julia, and I felt an undeniable surge of sexual excitement. All of my life experiences seemed to come together at once and I *knew* I'd discovered the core of myself. I finally saw all that I'd been feeling in a new, sexual light, and I found the word for myself: lesbian.

I could go on endlessly about Julia, how much this first love meant to me, how I wanted to spend the rest of my life with her, how she was intelligent, athletic, absolutely beautiful, and completely unattainable. My first love never became anything more than a sweet fantasy that filled my mind throughout high school. Once I kissed her on the cheek — a terribly brave gesture, because social kissing, even at Christmas, was something that took place in another world.

Years later, I wondered why I was so frightened of telling her how I felt. I thought for a while that it was racism, since she was black and I was white and our worlds outside the classroom were strictly segregated. I'm honest enough to admit that that might have been part of the reason, but most of it was that I was afraid. I was lonely and refused to risk having the one and only fantasy that kept me company pulled out from under me.

Just before we started college, I did come out to her. But I didn't have the guts to tell her then that I loved *her*, Julia, the woman who was still to me the most beautiful, gentle, desirable woman on earth, and who'd also become deeply entrenched in the "cool" crowd, smoking weed and sleeping with men. Seven years after our knees first touched, I ran into her on a bus, and at the end of a long ride I told her that she was my first love. We bravely hugged each other during the middle of rush hour in a rather rough section of downtown.

The very first time I actually *told* anyone — the first time I ever said the word "lesbian" out loud — was completely unplanned. I was seventeen, in my senior year, and I'd landed an incredible job as one of the editors of a student-operated tabloid newspaper. We were the *crème de la crème* of up-and-coming high school journalists pulled predominantly from the best schools.

We, six other student editors and our very hip adult editor-in-chief, were in the midst of a pre-brainstorm session lunch. I was seated across the table from a man who was to become a long-time friend (and would later come out himself) retelling a stunt pulled at school: someone had pasted a "Kiss Me I'm Gay" sign on someone else's back. Our very liberal editor-in-chief said rather quietly but firmly, "We don't think those kind of jokes are funny because one of our staff is gay."

I just about crawled under the table. "How did she know about me?" Then, as my internal panic subsided, I realized: there must be *someone else* who's gay. *I'm not the only one!!*

I looked cautiously at each person at the table and placed my bet on a thin, short-haired, rather butch-looking woman, our photographic editor. Later I found out that I was wrong; Katie was from an avante garde family and was just a couple of years ahead of the androgynous look. The point is, I *had* to know who it was, and since I couldn't be sure by guessing, the only way I thought I could find out was by revealing myself.

In the car on the way back to the office, I told our editor-in-chief that I was a lesbian. She nearly drove the car onto the curb and gave me the most unequivocally positive response I've ever gotten, particularly when she found out that it was the first time I'd told anyone.

When we reached the office she introduced me to David, the other gay person on the staff. He later introduced me to gay theater in Minneapolis and long soul-searching talks unlike any I'd had before. The editor assured me that everyone on staff was tolerant, if not supportive, and I decided to make an announcement to get my coming out off on the right track. Impulsively, I stood on a chair to announce my lesbianism, an honesty equalled only by marching in the New York Pride Day Parade. After our meeting was over, as we were leaving the building with the sun setting dramatically, David bid me farewell by proclaiming "Welcome out!" It was an extremely positive, unusual, and good start

Like a snowball rolling down a mountain, I kept coming out to the important people in my life. During one of our soul-searching talks on the telephone, David convinced me that I should tell my parents. He planned on telling his, and he knew his mother, who loved him very much, would take it well. Besides, being closeted to your own parents smacks of dishonesty that shouldn't exist in a good parent-child relationship.

In another bravado gesture, I asked David to hold the phone. I walked into the living room where my parents were watching *Charlie's Angels*, turned down the sound on the TV and said, "Mom, Dad, I have to tell you something. I'm a lesbian."

My father replied, "Bullshit. Turn the sound back up."

I told them I knew it was difficult for them to accept and asked them to think about it for a while, and that I'd talk about it later. Then I high-tailed it back to the phone and the safety of my room. Talking to David then gave me the courage to go back out and face my parents twenty minutes later.

Mom, Dad and I talked for a long time, and we cried a little, too. But they eventually reaffirmed what I'd always known: that they love me very deeply and will always be my staunchest supporters. After much pleading and cajoling three years later, they marched in my first Gay Pride Parade with me, carrying a sign that said WE LOVE OUR LESBIAN DAUGHTER. Appropriately, that year, 1981, the theme of the parade was "Love in Action." Later, Mom said she had no regrets about it — except that it took three days for her girdle to dry out.

Since I had all this unbelievable support, one would expect me to be unrealistically happy, but I wasn't. I was out to myself, my co-workers, and my parents, but I had yet to actually have a relationship with another woman. I was still incredibly lonely, and wanted to become a part of the city's lesbian community. At first it didn't seem necessary to come out into the lesbian community, but in reality it was. I had to assert myself and find a place to fit in.

There were no lesbian bars in Minneapolis, and there was one women's bar in St. Paul, but it was out of the question since it was more than two hours away by bus. There was, however, an alcohol-free space called "The Women's Coffeehouse." After discovering it, it took me about a year to find the nerve to go there. In the meantime, I found the Amazon Bookstore, my refuge from the overwhelmingly straight world. It supplied me with tons of reading materials and lesbian-positive images, but it was hardly a social nucleus for me.

My experience in "the lesbian community" got progressively more negative because everyone, myself included, was uncomfortable with my young age. When I did make it to the Women's Coffeehouse I was shunned because I was a stranger. Everyone was already quite well-organized into cliques. I searched on until I discovered a building called the Lesbian Resource Center, and I joined the coming out group. I thought it wasn't appropriate since I was already *out*, but it was a way to meet other lesbians. Unfortunately, the friendships didn't last too long. As a first-year college student, I had little in common with women concerned about their careers, house-buying, and their long-term relationships with lovers.

I tried fitting into the "politically correct" community. I joined the brand-new *Lesbian Inciter* newspaper collective. At the meetings, I was confronted with the process of consensus, the ideals of separatism, more ageism, and the politics of class.

But I was still very much on the outside, and *lonely*. After meetings, the women broke up into cliques and ignored me. At that point, it would have been more meaningful if someone had asked me if I'd had a nice day than about my experience in the patriarchal university. But no one ever asked me if I'd had a nice day, or how my classes were.

Then I joined a small single lesbian's group which was composed of the few *Lesbian Inciter* women who weren't in monogamous couples, and none of *them* under forty. Most of them were into discussing their unfulfilling, short-lived relationships. And there I was, still looking for my first one! I made the decision to leave that group the night one woman said she didn't masturbate because it just wasn't as good, wasn't as "fulfilling" as having a partner. Speaking as one who'd done nothing but, during the break I put my arm around her and whispered, "Diane, about masturbation: you must not be doing it right."

Years later, I heard about something called "internalized homophobia," which is like learning to hate yourself and distrust those around you because society hates you. Phobias are fears. Straight people who fear queers are dangerous enough, but when we begin to fear each other and consequently ourselves, then we create a divided community open to only a select few. Homophobia makes "them" want to lock us away from "them", but it also makes *us* want to lock *us* away from ourselves and each other.

I consider myself lucky. I am supported and loved by the many important people in my life, friends and family, and in retrospect, I can almost understand why I wasn't welcomed with open arms into a community where I felt I belonged. Ultimately I did have my first sexual experience, and have even had a couple of monogamous relationships. I moved to Baltimore, where I'm currently living, and found a "new" lesbian community completely different from that of Minneapolis. I've heard that the Minneapolis community is much changed now, and includes dykes even younger than I was.

Ironically, Minneapolis does seem friendlier now that I'm living in Baltimore. It could be because the lesbian community has changed, or because as I age I become more comfortable with myself. Or it could have something to do with my last visit, when I seduced one of the most beautiful women in the Twin Cities area. Most likely it's because I'm learning that there is no "right" or "wrong" to coming out. My lesbianism is an integral part of my individuality, and each time I assert myself I come out, sooner or later. My coming out story is my life story, which is harder to end than it was to begin. Since coming out is a lifelong process, there's always the possibility of a new beginning.

Candyce Rusk
Boston, Massachusetts

One Sunday

I remember the warm Sunday afternoon distinctly. It was in the mid-sixties — I don't clearly remember the year — but oh, that hot afternoon! I lived in a small midwestern town along the shores of Lake Michigan. Pam, the fifteen-year-old blonde *femme fatale* of my neighborhood was with me in my parents' guestroom. I was about thirteen, and all fire and tomboy, hating hair curlers, and playing "Kick the Can" with the boys.

Pam had big blue eyes, a full toothy smile, and wore her newly developed figure with a definite pride. "Kick the Can" didn't interest her, even though she was a fast runner. I was, frankly, on the edge of a strong attraction to her, and very shy.

Shades and curtains drawn, we lay on the divan amidst popcorn and newspapers, eagerly waiting for the world premiere of *The Three Stooges Go to the Moon*. As the opening credits rolled, Pammy turned to me, fluttering her eyes. She placed her newly polished pink fingernails on my thigh. I feigned indifference, though excited by this unusual move. My mind flipped to Annette Funicello, the cutest and best-developed Mouseketeer. I had a strange feeling about Annette — a feeling I know now as attraction, and, well, adolescent lust. But here was Pam, her fingers running down my leg, slowly.

She turned. "If you had to be a Stooge, which one would you be?" Her voice chimed in my head.

"Oh, Moe," I answered quickly. "He doesn't get hit as much and he's the big shot."

"Really now, Moe, that hair," she replied. "At least yours is blonde." Her arm smoothly encircled my shoulder. Moving slow as molasses, her fingers moved up my neck.

As the Stooges raced around on the screen, my young heart thudded loudly in my chest. I closed my eyes and hoped my brothers and sister wouldn't barge in.

"Where's the newspaper?" Pam asked, suddenly moving away. She grabbed the paper off the floor, her madras pants pulling tight and revealing her smooth upper backside. I thought briefly of temptation and sin, being a Catholic, and then pushed it from my mind.

"See this?" Pam's long finger was fixed on a movie ad from a James Bond film. A semi-nude model was reclining seductively on a couch, her head close to the floor, her breasts on the edge, pointing majestically upward.

"Yes, I see it," I said gruffly. "What about it?"

"She's beautiful, don't you think?" questioned Pam.

"Sure," I answered, struggling to remain cool. What was she getting at anyway? According to the nuns at school, anybody who saw a James Bond film was a "pagan." Pam was a Lutheran and obviously going to Hell, unless I could convert her to the Catholic Church. Given the way things were progressing, that seemed highly unlikely.

"Let's play 'James Bond.'" She faced me fully, her chest heaving with excitement. "You . . . you be James Bond, and I'll be her — the girlfriend." She reached gently for my glasses and slid them under the divan. The world went soft around the edges. Squinting, I watched as Pam's arms crossed in front of her. She pulled off her sweater. Such a ribcage! And her bra! All lace. I'd only seen bras like that on the mannequins at Penny's Department Store downtown. Certainly I didn't own one. I was glad she was playing the girlfriend — she was so well equipped for the part.

"Now," she got up and opened a closet door, "a gown, or a robe." Pam pulled out a gaudy black negligée someone had given my mother as a joke. She put it on. The top half of Pam was all woman. The bottom had pants which stuck out merrier than twin plaid Christmas trees. Still, I was duly impressed.

"All right." She moved, standing directly in front of me. "You go into the closet and act like you just came back from a spy mission." Getting up, I gave her a wide-eyed look, fully aware that this was far more serious than our usual pretend games.

Once inside, I heard the muffles from the Three Stooges soundtrack. Pam was positioning herself with great pains on the couch, judging from the sound of things. I felt silly and flushed in the dark closet. A strong pulsing of blood wound its way through my body. Would Pam want me to kiss her? I didn't have any practice, except when I kissed my own wrist.

Finally she called me out, "All right James . . . Mr. Bond . . . come in please." I filled my chest with air, simulating a burly strength. I wouldn't find out till years later that Bond was suave and slim.

I strode out of the closet, surprised and deeply delighted at Pam's invitation. Her gown was open, her breasts pointing majestically upward. I froze, unsure.

"On top of me," Pam breathed, air stuck in her throat. I lay on top of her . . . just like that. Pam's upside-down face was turning red. "Come on, dummy." I responded to that request. I lay down on her, feeling her warm curves and bones. My face was in line with her breasts. Pam sighed. I thought I was squishing her.

"Now kiss them." Plural. That meant two. That meant her breasts. Oh my God. I bent down, my lips nuzzling along the edges of her lace bra. I was aware of their soft sponginess. "Now pull it down," Pam urged. I tugged gently and her breasts jiggled, waiting to be set free. Sympathetically, Pam pulled her bra up. I stared at her nipples, such a light soft pink. I felt them looking at me. "Kiss them." I kissed. So soft. So warm. So Pam. "Now circle them with your finger." Slowly I outlined her breasts, shuddering, truly amazed at the sensuality of this game. My own breasts were tingling, as was the lower half of my body. I wanted her hand there, touching me. Pam moaned and we melted into each other.

From out of nowhere, my little brother shouted, "Hey, open

up you guys!" I guiltily slid off of Pam, sideways. She fell to the floor, her bare half disappearing from me. "I wanna watch the movie, you TV hogs!" My sibling screamed from the far side of the world. Pam, flushed and insulted, hissed at me, "James Bond doesn't have any brothers!" She quickly adjusted her bra, and removed herself from my mother's nightgown. As she grabbed for her sweater, my heart sank. I realized I had crossed some border and was forever changed. I'd had a confusing but sweet glimpse at sensuality, the gentle give and take of desire.

Later that night, the sultry day became evening and the sun turned a deep red. Pam and I rode our bikes to the Dairy Queen on Main Street. I insisted on buying her a cherry-coated vanilla cone, perhaps because it reminded me of her soft, soft breasts.

I didn't know that Pam would turn quickly to boys after our encounter, excitedly relaying to me stories of her sexual progressions. I stayed spinning in a state of desire for her, ready and waiting for another cue that never came.

Years later, when both of us were in college, I visited Pam at her apartment for the weekend. Lying on the same double mattress on the floor, she turned to me. "Ever make it with another girl?" she asked off-handedly. It dawned on me that the rite of passion we had shared was buried somewhere in her subconscious. "I've fooled around a bit," I sighed, "but I guess it wasn't serious." We turned from each other then, our sharing forever sealed. Listening to a Buffalo Springfield album, my mind wandered back to the old neighborhood. Hard rocket baseballs, "Kick the Can," the Three Stooges, the Beatles. How many people can associate an erotic memory with the Three Stooges? I can — that warm Sunday afternoon with Pam.

Nancy Wechsler
Somerville, Massachusetts

Front Page News

The most recent wave of the gay liberation movement, while not responsible for anything as dramatic as saving my life, is responsible for my sanity. I went to public school in Levittown, New York, when girls were to be girls, and boys were to be boys. It was a time when dresses or skirts were mandatory, when girls were supposed to care about how they looked, and care about what boys thought of them. I fudged it through elementary school by wearing pants under my skirts — but if by sixth grade that was getting a bit tough, by seventh grade there was no way I could pull it off. I settled for changing right after school, into more comfortable clothes I kept in my gym locker.

As soon as I learned to talk and walk I engaged my parents in constant battles over what I was willing to wear, and how I would or would not behave. In a world where girls were feminine and less athletic than the boys, I was as good at most sports as any of the boys in my neighborhood. I walked tough, played rough, and engaged in spitting competitions with my neighbors.

While part of me thought I might grow up and get married, I wondered how I would ever survive in a world where women wore dresses and makeup. Would I go through some magical transformation? As the years went by, I realized no such transformation was taking place. I pictured myself growing up to be the only woman who wore pants all her life. Though I could not imagine giving in to societal pressures, neither could I project the shape my life would take.

Those early pre-women's liberation, pre-gay liberation days were difficult. Feeling alone, isolated, ugly, and an outcast with other outcasts as my friends, these years took their toll. Not a day passed during which I was not harassed as I walked to school or the store. Catcalls and chants of "Are you a boy or a girl?" hounded me constantly.

While I "felt up" another girl in the back seat of our family car, and pined away over movie actresses (Julie Christie and Geraldine Chaplain particularly caught my eye in "Dr. Zhivago"), it didn't occur to me that I was a lesbian. I think my mother had her fears, but never mentioned them to me until I brought it up years later. In the pre-Stonewall days of my elementary and secondary school years, I'm not sure I knew lesbians existed. In high school, I discussed Camus, Kafka, Shakespeare, the Vietnam War, and the Civil Rights Movement with my close friends, many of whom also came out years later, but we didn't manage to help each other realize we were queer. We lacked the necessary information about sex, and lived in a community that would not have enthusiastically received news of our desires. Mostly we suppressed our sexual desires. I channeled mine into athletics, while my friends devoted themselves to Drama Club, Orchestra, or school work.

My greatest joys as a youngster revolved around sports. I was very lucky that our junior and senior high school had comprehensive women's sports programs. I played on almost every girls' varsity team: tennis, basketball, volleyball, softball, and field hockey. I became good friends with my gym teacher, who taught me to ski, and along with my math teacher and a group of five or six boys, we all went together on weekend ski trips to New England.

But still, with all the joys and recognitions that athletics brought me, I could not shake the feeling that something was wrong with me. I had grown up listening to my mother expound on the wonders of sex, about how it was one of the most beautiful things in the world. When at an early age I asked her about masturbation, she smiled and told me, "Oh, everyone does that, it's fine." In such a liberated family, what was my problem? I could not imagine feeling the joy of sexual excitement my mother described. When I finally did sleep with some men, it was at best boring, at worst physically painful. My mother's words rang in my ears as I lay on my back — dry, in pain, wishing it were over. The year I slept with men was the only time in my life that I got up and out of bed early in the morning — anything to limit the possibility of having more sex. No relationship lasted more than two or three months.

In September 1970, I picked up a book called *Sisterhood is Powerful*, edited by Robin Morgan. Although it contained very little lesbian content, it didn't really take much to open my eyes to the fact that I was a lesbian. I sought out all other literature of the early women's and gay movements, including *Women Identified Women*, a pamphlet by Radicalesbians, and joined a consciousness-raising group. Finally I felt part of a larger movement challenging the sex role stereotyping and confinement that had plagued me.

I don't remember hearing about the Stonewall Rebellion in 1969, but I do remember the very beginnings of gay activism in Ann Arbor, Michigan, where I was attending college. An out lesbian ran for student government on a slate with several radicals. A chapter of the Gay Liberation Front (GLF) was formed, and later some lesbians split to form Radicalesbians (RL). A few years after that GAWK — the Gay Awareness Women's Kollective — was formed and I joined. GAWK organized consciousness-raising groups, did public outreach and educationals around being a lesbian, and participated in demonstrations. In the early seventies, Ann Arbor had a very organized left, a small but active gay liberation movement, and a strong but disorganized feminist movement. There were CR groups, women's caucuses of groups like the Ann Arbor Tenants Union, and other left groups, and a women's newspaper. I was involved in many of these activities and remember that in addition to talking about the sexism within mixed left organizations, we worked on issues such as day care, abortion, and other reproductive rights. While there was a sense

of being involved in the beginnings of a movement, it was a movement without the structure and culture of what we might today
loosely term our community. I remember the night a member of
our lesbian CR group told us that she had an incredible record to
play for us ... and she put on the first album of lesbian music,
Lavender Jane Loves Women by Alex Dobkin and Kay Gard-
ner. Lesbian novels were few and hard to come by. A friend
loaned me her incredible collection of lesbian trash from the fifties.
The University established offices of gay and lesbian concerns and
women's concerns, and they served as drop-in centers.

In those early years, I didn't experience the clash many fem-
inists experience between the left and the gay or women's movement. It was actually through the socialist group I belonged to that
I first met openly gay people and attended gay liberation demonstrations. My leftist friends from that time, many of whom are still
friends and are politically active today, immediately chose to join
in and support the rebelliousness and spunkiness of the gay movement. We all believed that challenging societal norms was what
both the New Left and the gay movement were about.

While I knew some members of GLF and RL, I was rooted in
the left, where most of my friends were straight. One year I lived
with nine of my cohorts from the Ann Arbor Tenants Union. I told
some of them I thought I was a lesbian. They were supportive, but
since they were straight it didn't give me the chance to explore, or
take action regarding the part of me that was beginning to think I
was queer. I wrote in my journal over and over, "I am a lesbian, I
am a lesbian, I am a lesbian," hoping it would sink in and become
comprehensible. Then I tore it to shreds and threw it out. It was
1970 and I was scared. My worst fear was that maybe I wasn't
really a lesbian. Maybe sex with women wouldn't feel good either,
maybe I was frigid, doomed to an existence devoid of the wondrous sexual energy my mother had taught me about. My fear
kept me locked inside myself for three years, until in 1973 I was
dragged out by a friend who not only took me to lesbian parties
and introduced me around, but gave me my first passionate kiss.

In 1971 I graduated from the University of Michigan. I
became coordinator of the city's Human Rights-Radical Independent Party, (HRP) a third party that had begun the year before
with the merger of several radical socialist student groups.

While originally skeptical of the idea of socialists participating in electoral politics, even third party politics, I became convinced that this was an important area to work within. With the slowing down of the Vietnam War, and the subsequent slowing down of the student movement, HRP gave the Ann Arbor left a chance to reach out beyond the student community with a broad platform for social change. HRP was as committed to organizing and participating in demonstrations and strikes as it was committed to running in city, county, and school board elections. Having a radical third party that ran against Democrats and Republicans alike allowed us the opportunity to educate people about the similarities between the two major parties, and particularly about the historical role of the Democratic Party in coopting and diffusing mass movements for social change.

In 1972, still pondering the questions of whether or not I was a lesbian, I was urged to run for city council from Ward 2, where HRP felt fairly confident it could win. I had spent a good deal of time trying to find other candidates, as I lacked the self-confidence to run. Noticing that men in the party seemed not to have that problem, I began thinking of running to challenge my own socialization as a woman.

I had many qualms, fears, and questions about running for office. In addition to my insecurities, I wondered how it would change my life. Among my many qualms about running was the fact that I thought I was a lesbian, but I hadn't yet slept with a woman. Only my good friends in the party knew I thought I was queer. Did this mean I had to get up in front of three or four hundred people at our nominating convention and say, "Look, there is something you might want to know before you nominate me. I might be a dyke"? I wasn't ready to make that statement. I talked it over with other HRP activists, my friends and housemates, and finally went to talk to my friends in GLF for support and advice. I told them if they believed I should get up at our meeting and say I was gay, I would. Was I gay if I hadn't yet even slept with a woman? Would running as an openly gay candidate be truthful? GLF's response was supportive and nonjudgemental. They told me, "Look, you don't know if you are gay or not, you don't have to come out. We know you support us, and that you've been at every gay demonstration and every picket line. We trust you. You'd have a better chance to get elected if you didn't come out, and we'd like you to get elected."

Looking back, I feel mixed about their advice. Perhaps I needed someone to help me work through my questions so that I would be able to come out, even though I hadn't yet had lesbian sex. I am sure the party would have nominated me either way. But as I am writing this, over ten years later, I realize that I can't really fault GLF for not being able to do for me what I was not ready to do for myself. So while I did not announce in front of all HRP that I thought I was queer, I did make a promise to myself that *every* time I spoke, every debate, every talk show, every door-to-door canvas, I would mention the gay liberation part of our platform. That was a promise I kept, and so in looking back on my campaign I feel no shame.

GLF was supportive during the entire campaign, and during my two years on city council. It was during our first year on the council, before either of us were publicly out, that Jerry DeGrieck (HRP-1st Ward) and I introduced and got passed an HRP-written amendment to the city's human rights ordinance banning discrimination based on sexual preference.

When we came out publicly — at a council meeting during our second year — it was front page news. We took the occasion of a visit to council by the Chief of Police to question him about the lack of enforcement of the human rights ordinance, and his failure to educate his officers about the ordinance. The amount of hate mail that Jerry and I regularly received jumped, and mine was now filled with epithets against my being a Jew, a commie, *and* a queer — an obviously unacceptable condition to some of the people of Ann Arbor and surrounding communities.

Despite the hate mail, I experienced coming out publicly as a exhilarating and liberating experience. It literally gave me the energy to finish my second year on the council even though I was also dealing with my mother's slow death from cancer. A new period had begun for me of intense crushes, passionate sex, wonderful beginnings, and difficult breakups. I learned about what turned me on, and who turned me on. I was like an adolescent and I had a lot of catching up to do. I walked around Ann Arbor with a high I had never experienced before or since — I had finally found and accepted myself, and I had found and become a part of a gay and lesbian community.

Having two openly queer radicals on the city council made for some lively times. GLF and HRP (which was by this time approximately one-third gay and lesbian) organized demonstrations which closed down city council meetings as we demanded public space, recognition, and an understanding of our politics. Far from the respectable image some gay politicians today would like us all to have, we raised hell and did not try to pretend we were the same as everyone else.

My experience of being so openly gay in Ann Arbor affected choices I made later on when I moved to Boston in 1974. Taking a job in a social service agency in Somerville, I was discouraged from coming out by all those around me. But coming out at work, in political groups, and in my neighborhood was important to me, as well as being important politically. Closets provide only a false sense of safety. Coming out is still one of the most important acts a gay person can make. I've always urged my friends to push the limits of what they think might be possible, to give some serious thought to coming out at work, at school, and to their family.

I got involved in the gay and lesbian liberation movement not because of some altruistic notion that it would make a better world, and not simply because I had an analysis which confirmed that gay and lesbian liberation was a threat to the nuclear family, and, therefore, capitalism. I got involved because it was what was needed to make a world in which I could live and grow, and so that things would be better for those who came after me. I did not "come out in the women's movement." I have always been a lesbian. But it was the women's and the gay and lesbian liberation movements which gave me a name for what I was.

The women's movement and the gay and lesbian liberation movement also allowed me some space outside the confines of my sex role. Since it is these broader politics which engaged me to begin with — not simply a desire for "gay rights" — it is these politics which feed and nourish me now. And with the re-emergence in the eighties of strong pressures once again to conform to feminine stereotypes, it is these broader politics of gay and lesbian liberation and their challenge to the norms of the dominant culture, the nuclear family, "normal sexuality," and traditional gender roles, that we so desperately need to articulate now.

About the Contributors

Angelus (Angela Bowen) writes, "My given name is Angelus. When I started studying Latin in the seventh grade, I discovered that the 'us' ending was masculine, and I decided to change my name to Angela. For fifty years, I've been Angela. With this piece, I take back my given name as my pen name."

Nona Caspers is a performance artist and writer in Minneapolis, Minnesota. Her poetry and fiction has appeared in *Hurricane, Alice, Negative Capability, Plainswoman,* and other publications. She was raised in rural Minnesota surrounded by cows, crosses, blood sausage, and fried potatoes.

Emma Joy Crone is the editor of *A Web of Crones*, a periodical by, for and about older women. She lives on Hornby Island, British Columbia, and is working on her biography.

Rhonda Gilliam writes, "Born in Southern California, I was raised and educated in rural West Texas. At thirty-six, I have found and committed my love to a wonderful woman and am pursuing my Master's degree in English and Creative Writing."

Jewelle Gomez has written book reviews for *Belles Lettres, The Village Voice,* and *The New York Times.* She is the author of two collections of poetry and a forthcoming vampire novel, *The Gilda Stories.*

Pamela Gordon writes, "I live in Maine with my lover Barbara and we are very happy. I do advertising for Maine's gay and lesbian newspaper, and the two of us run an antique business together."

Lisa Gravesen writes, "I am a twenty-seven-year-old aquarian toolmaker who likes music, sports, camping, and tales of elderly women. Although my good friends consider me crazier than hell, they are my most valued treasure and I love them all."

Gillian Hanscombe was born in Melbourne, Australia in 1945. Her work covers a wide range of creativity, including poetry, polemic, journalism and fiction, such as the novel *Between Friends*. She currently lives and writes by the sea in Devon.

Linda Heal writes, "I'm currently underemployed in Madison, Wisconsin, which is teeming with lesbians and creative haircuts. Recently my lover became my life partner in a ceremony that included lots of music, dancing, trees, and grass. My mom was my best woman."

Sarah Holmes is a publicist, writer, and activist who lives in Jamaica Plain, Massachusetts.

Marcie Just is a resident of Colorado, living on the banks of the Roaring Fork River. She shares her home with her love, Traci, and her three feline companions, Ishi, Sakti, and Gandolf. She is an astrologer, herbalist, and free-lance writer.

Carol Lemieux is a writer and artist living in Medford, Massachusetts. Her artwork has been exhibited in the Boston area and she is currently working on her first novel.

Andrea Freud Loewenstein came out fifteen years ago, and is the author of one novel, *This Place*. She is now completing a novel for young adults and a collection of short stories. After many fulfilling years in adult education, she's ready to teach in a university, and she is working on a doctoral thesis to try to make this happen. She lives with her lover in Jamaica Plain, Massachusetts.

Other books of interest from
ALYSON PUBLICATIONS

Don't miss our FREE BOOK offer at the end of this section.

☐ **DEAR SAMMY: Letters from Gertrude Stein and Alice B. Toklas,** by Samuel M. Steward, $8.00. As a young man, Samuel M. Steward journeyed to France to meet the two women he so admired. It was the beginning of a long friendship. Here he combines his fascinating memoirs of Toklas and Stein with photos and more than a hundred of their letters.

☐ **LONG TIME PASSING: Lives of Older Lesbians,** edited by Marcy Adelman, $8.00. Here, in their own words, women talk about age-related concerns: the fear of losing a lover; the experiences of being a lesbian in the 1940s and 1950s; and issues of loneliness and community.

☐ **MURDER IS MURDER IS MURDER,** by Samuel M. Steward, $7.00. Gertrude Stein and Alice B. Toklas go sleuthing through the French countryside, attempting to solve the mysterious disappearance of their neighbor, the father of their handsome gardener. A new and very different treat from the author of the Phil Andros stories.

☐ **WORLDS APART,** edited by Camilla Decarnin, Eric Garber and Lyn Paleo, $8.00. Today's generation of science fiction writers has created a wide array of futuristic gay characters. The s-f stories collected here present adventure, romance, and excitement; and maybe some genuine alternatives for our future.

☐ **ONE TEENAGER IN TEN: Writings by gay and lesbian youth,** edited by Ann Heron, $4.00. One teenager in ten is gay; here, twenty-six young people tell their stories: of coming to terms with being different, of the decision how — and whether — to tell friends and parents, and what the consequences were.

☐ **THE TWO OF US,** by Larry Uhrig, $7.00. The author draws on his years of counseling with gay people to give some down-to-earth advice about what makes a relationship work. He gives special emphasis to the religious aspects of gay unions.

☐ **LIFETIME GUARANTEE,** by Alice Bloch, $7.00. Here is the personal and powerfully-written chronicle of a woman faced with the impending death of her sister from cancer, at the same time that she must also face her family's reaction to her lesbianism.

☐ **IRIS,** by Janine Veto, $7.00. When Iris and Dee meet in Hawaii, they both know that this is the relationship they have each been looking for; all they want is to live together on this island paradise forever. But the world has other plans, and Iris is forced to flee to a desolate Greek island. When they are united, Iris and Dee find that their love must now face a formidable foe if it is to survive.

☐ **A FEMINIST TAROT,** by Sally Miller Gearhart and Susan Rennie, $7.00. The first tarot book to emerge from the women's movement, with interpretations of tarot cards that reflect women's experiences in contemporary society.

☐ **THE LAVENDER COUCH,** by Marny Hall, $8.00. Here is a guide to the questions that should be considered by lesbians or gay men considering therapy or already in it: How do you choose a good therapist? What kind of therapy is right for you? When is it time to leave therapy?

☐ **THE LAW OF RETURN,** by Alice Bloch, $9.00. The widely-praised novel of a woman who, returning to Israel, regains her Jewish heritage while also claiming her voice as a woman and as a lesbian. "Clear, warm, haunting and inspired" writes Phyllis Chesler. "I want to read everything Alice Bloch writes," adds Grace Paley.

☐ **COMING TO POWER: Writings and graphics on lesbian S/M,** edited by Samois, $9.00. Few issues have divided the lesbian-feminist community as much as that of S/M practices among lesbians; here are essays, stories, pictures and personal testimony from members of Samois, the San Francisco lesbian-feminist S/M group.

☐ **DANCER DAWKINS AND THE CALIFORNIA KID,** by Willyce Kim, $6.00. Dancer Dawkins would like to just sit back and view life from behind a pile of hotcakes. But her lover, Jessica Riggins, has fallen into the clutches of Fatin Satin Aspen, and something must be done. Meanwhile, Little Willie Gutherie of Bangor, Maine, renames herself The California Kid, stocks up on Rubbles Dubble bubble gum, and heads west. When this crew collides in San Francisco, what can be expected? Just about anything. . . .

☐ **DEAD HEAT,** by Willyce Kim, $7.00. Dancer and the crew meet up for an all-new adventure involving Vinny 'The Skull', horce racing, and a kidnapped gypsy, but the result is one fast-paced, entertaining story you'll read again and again.

☐ **LEGENDE,** by Jeannine Allard, $6.00. Sometime in the last century, two women living on the coast of France, in Brittany, loved each other. They had no other models for such a thing, so one of them posed as a man for most of their life together. This legend is still told in Brittany; from it, Jeannine Allard has created a hauntingly beautiful story of two women in love.

☐ **TALK BACK! A gay person's guide to media action,** $4.00. When were you last outraged by prejudiced media coverage of gay people? Chances are it hasn't been long. This short, highly readable book tells how you, in surprisingly little time, can do something about it.

☐ **CHOICES,** by Nancy Toder, $8.00. This popular novel about lesbian love depicts the joy, passion, conflicts and intensity of love between women as Nancy Toder conveys the fear and confusion of a woman coming to terms with her sexual and emotional attraction to other women.

☐ **WANDERGROUND,** by Sally Miller Gearhart, $7.00. Here are stories of the hill women, who combine the control of mind and matter with a sensuous adherence to women's realities and history. A lesbian classic.

☐ **THE PEARL BASTARD,** by Lillian Halegua, $4.00. Frankie is fifteen when she leaves her large, suffocating Catholic family. Here, with painful innocence and acute vision, she tells the story of her sudden entry into a harsh maturity.

☐ **THE CRYSTAL CURTAIN,** by Sandy Bayer, $8.00. Stephanie Nowland had felt the power, even as a child — the power to see what was hidden, to sense the future. She used the power to help others.

Now a crazed, sadistic killer wants revenge on the woman who sent him to prison. He wants to kill her lover, Marian, too. Images of both women's deaths fill his thoughts.

Stephanie can see them there.

☐ **A HISTORY OF SHADOWS,** by Robert C. Reinhart, $7.00. A fascinating look at gay life during the Depression, the war years, the McCarthy witchhunts, and the sixties — through the eyes of four men who were friends during those forty years.

☐ **UNBROKEN TIES: Lesbian Ex-Lovers,** by Carol Becker, Ph.D., $8.00. Lesbian relationships with ex-lovers are complex and unusual ways of building alternative families and social networks. Carol Becker's interviews with numerous pairs of ex-lovers tell the trauma of breaking-up, the stages of recovery, and the differing ways of maintaining close emotional connections with former lovers.

Get this book free!

Frances and Meg were friends in school years ago; now Frances is a married housewife while Meg is a lesbian involved in progressive politics. Through letters written between these women and their friends, Gillian Hanscombe weaves an engrossing story of women loving women, while exploring many vital lesbian and feminist issues.

If you order at least three other books from us, you may request a FREE copy of *Between Friends*. (See order form on next page.)

☐ **WE CAN ALWAYS CALL THEM BULGARIANS: The Emergence of Lesbians and Gay Men on the American Stage,** by Kaier Curtin, $10.00. Despite police raids and censorship laws, many plays with gay or lesbian roles met with success on Broadway during the first half of this century. Here, Kaier Curtin documents the reactions of theatergoers, critics, clergymen, politicians and law officers to the appearance of these characters. Illustrated with photos from actual performances.

To get these books:

Ask at your favorite bookstore for the books listed here. You may also order by mail. Just fill out the coupon below, or use your own paper if you prefer not to cut up this book.

GET A FREE BOOK! When you order any three books listed here at the regular price, you may request a *free* copy of *Between Friends*.

— — — — — — — — — — — — — — — — — —

Enclosed is $_____ for the following books. (Add $1.00 postage when ordering just one book; if you order two or more, we'll pay the postage.)

1. _____

2. _____

3. _____

4. _____

5. _____

☐ Send a free copy of *Between Friends* as offered above. I have ordered at least three other books.

name: _____

address: _____

city: _____ state: _____ zip: _____

ALYSON PUBLICATIONS
Dept. H-42, 40 Plympton St., Boston, Mass. 02118

This offer expires Dec. 31, 1990. After that date, please write for current catalog.